Henry Alfred Harding

Analysis of Form as Displayed in Beethoven's Thirty-two Pianoforte Sonatas

With a Description of the Form of Each Movement for the Use of Students

Henry Alfred Harding

Analysis of Form as Displayed in Beethoven's Thirty-two Pianoforte Sonatas
With a Description of the Form of Each Movement for the Use of Students

ISBN/EAN: 9783744797993

Printed in Europe, USA, Canada, Australia, Japan

Cover: Foto ©Thomas Meinert / pixelio.de

More available books at **www.hansebooks.com**

SEVENTEENTH THOUSAND.

NOVELLO'S

MUSIC PRIMERS AND EDUCATIONAL SERIES.

Edited by Sir JOHN STAINER and Sir C. HUBERT H. PARRY.

ANALYSIS OF FORM

AS DISPLAYED IN

BEETHOVEN'S
THIRTY-TWO PIANOFORTE SONATAS

WITH A DESCRIPTION OF THE FORM OF EACH MOVEMENT

FOR THE USE OF STUDENTS

BY

H. A. HARDING
Mus. Doc., Oxon.

PRICE TWO SHILLINGS.
Paper Boards, Two Shillings and Sixpence.

This "Analysis of Form" contains the Answers to the 350 Questions upon the Form
and Tonality of Beethoven's Pianoforte Sonatas to be found in
Primer No. 57.
("Questions on Form," price 6d.)

London : NOVELLO AND COMPANY, Limited.
New York: THE H. W. GRAY CO., Sole Agents for the U.S.A.

PREFACE.

A LTHOUGH much has been written upon the poetical and romantic ideas contained in Beethoven's Pianoforte Sonatas, I am not aware that a complete analysis of each Sonata has ever been published. I hope, therefore, that this little work will prove useful to, and supply a want felt by, musical Students, to whom a thorough knowledge of the way in which Beethoven has treated the orthodox rules of form in these compositions cannot but be of the greatest benefit.

Bedford, 1889.   H. A. HARDING.

New Editions have afforded me the opportunity of reconstructing some parts of this Analysis, with the view of making it clearer to the Student. I have also adopted the more expressive names of "Ternary" for "Aria," and "Simple Binary" for "Modified Sonata Form." And in response to urgent requests, I have given alternate schemes for some of the movements, upon the form of which there are various opinions.

Bedford, 1901.   H. A. H.

INTRODUCTION.

A MODERN SONATA consists of 2, 3, or 4 movements :—
The 1st movement is generally written in " Sonata Form " (a).
The 2nd movement (slow) in " Ternary Form " (b).
The 3rd movement (Minuet and Trio) in " Ternary Form."
The 4th movement in " Rondo Form."
Some movements (though rarely) are written in "Air with Variations Form" and others in "Fugue Form."

SONATA FORM.

This Form is composed of three parts, which may be called the Enunciation, Development, and Recapitulation respectively; the following is a rough outline of each part :—

ENUNCIATION.	DEVELOPMENT. E.	RECAPITULATION. F.
1st Subject in tonic key, (A) followed by a Connecting Episode (Bridge Passage) modulating to the dominant key (B). 2nd Subject in dominant key, after which there is a (C) Coda ending in dominant key (D). Double bar and repeat (optional).	In this part the principal themes found in the Enunciation are developed. The modulations are arranged to lead back to tonic key.	1st Subject in tonic key, followed by the Connecting Episode, transposed so as to lead into tonic key (instead of dominant). 2nd Subject in tonic key, after which comes the Coda, which, of course, ends in tonic key.

A. The 1st subject ends with a full close (c) in the tonic key, but this rule is often disregarded—for instance, in Sonatas Nos. 1 and 19 the 1st subject of the 1st movement ends on a half-close (d); in No. 23 it ends on the dominant; and in No. 9 the end overlaps the entry of the Connecting Episode.

B. The Connecting Episode, sometimes called "The Bridge," consists of modulating passages, leading from the key of the 1st subject, to that of the 2nd subject; they may be formed upon the 1st subject, or consist of new ideas.

C. When the movement is in a major key, the 2nd subject is generally in the dominant key (when the movement is in a minor key, the 2nd subject is usually in the relative major key); but there are many instances where it occurs in other keys : see Sonatas Nos. 1, 2, 3, 14, 16, 17, 21, 23, 27, 29, 32. These exceptions also apply to the 2nd subject in Rondo Form. See Nos. 10, 19.

D. The Coda consists of a few passages confirming the full close in the dominant key.

E. The Development (Free Fantasia), which forms the second portion of the movement, contains "developments" of the themes enunciated in Part I. These developments should be of a "contrapuntal, canonical, imitative, or fugal kind." New ideas may be introduced to work in with previous material. This part should end by leading back to tonic key (the Development should not *begin* in tonic key).

F. The Recapitulation, or Third Part, consists of a repetition of the Enunciation; the second Subject, however, is transposed to tonic key, and the preceding Connecting Episode altered to lead to that key. The Coda is often prolonged, and sometimes contains new ideas.

(a). Sometimes called " Modern Binary," " Movement of Continuity," or " 1st Movement Form."
(b). Also called " Song Form," " Aria Form," " Simple Episodical Form."
(c). " Perfect Cadence."
(d). " Imperfect Cadence."

SIMPLE BINARY FORM (Miniature Sonata Form).*

This Form is divided into two parts :—

First Part   **Subject** in tonic key—often ending in dominant key (double bar, and repeat optional).

Second Part   Short development.
          Subject repeated, ending in tonic key.

When the movement is in a minor key the first part often ends in relative major key. It is easy to trace in this Form the germs of the Sonata Form—in fact, Simple Binary Form is often a miniature example of Sonata Form.

TERNARY FORM.*

As the name implies, this Form is in three parts :—

1st Part.	2nd Part.	3rd Part.
Subject in tonic key. Short development. Subject repeated, ending in tonic key (Simple Binary Form).	**New Subject** in new key. Short development. **New Subject** repeated on the same plan as Part I., but often leading back to dominant of tonic key.	Repetition of 1st Part (often varied).

RONDO FORM.

Rondo Form is divided into three parts :—

Part I.	Part II.	Part III.
1st **Subject** in tonic key. Connecting Episode. (Bridge Passage.) 2nd **Subject** in dominant key,† passages leading back to 1st **Subject** in original key.	3rd **Subject** in related key, or development of previous themes, leading to dominant of original key.	1st **Subject** in tonic key. Connecting Episode. (Bridge Passage.) 2nd **Subject** in tonic key, passages leading to 1st **Subject** in original key. Coda.

Sometimes in Rondo Form there is only one **Subject**, alternating with Episodes, and the scheme is as follows:—

Subject. Episode. Subject.	Episode.	Subject. Coda.

See Sonatas Nos. 7, 20, 24, 25, and 30.

AIR WITH VARIATIONS FORM

consists of a well-defined melody of definite length, followed by a series of "variations" upon it, the air appearing in "various kinds of figure and rhythm" and "in varied division and complication of parts, changes of harmony, with contrapuntal and even fugal treatment, provided the melodious order and phrasing is preserved throughout."‡

FUGUE FORM

is one of the strictest of musical forms. Its chief characteristic is, that the Subject enunciated at the commencement by one part is imitated by all the other parts in succession, contrapuntally.§

* See " Musical Form " (E. Prout) (Augener and Co.).
† See Note (C) Sonata Form.
‡ " Musical Forms " (Pauer) (Novello).
§ See " Fugue " (Higgs) (Novello) for a full description of Fugue Form.

CONTENTS.

SONATA No. 1.*

Op. 2, No. 1.

FIRST MOVEMENT.—"ALLEGRO," KEY OF F MINOR. SONATA FORM.

ENUNCIATION.	DEVELOPMENT.	RECAPITULATION.
1——9$^{(2)}$. 1st subject in F minor (tonic) A.	50$^{(4)}$—103$^{(1)}$. E.	103 — 110$^{(3)}$. 1st subject in original key.
9$^{(1)}$—21$^{(1)}$. Connecting episode. B.		110$^{(4)}$—121$^{(1)}$. Connecting episode. F.
21$^{(1)}$—42$^{(1)}$. 2nd subject in A♭ major. C.		121$^{(4)}$—142$^{(1)}$. 2nd subject in tonic key.
42$^{(3)}$—49$^{(1)}$. Coda. D.		142$^{(3)}$. Coda. G.
Double bar and repeat.		

SECOND MOVEMENT.—"ADAGIO," KEY OF F MAJOR. MODIFIED SONATA FORM.

ENUNCIATION.	DEVELOPMENT.	RECAPITULATION.
1 — 17$^{(2)}$. 1st subject in tonic key. A.	32. C.	33—48. 1st subject in original key. D.
17$^{(2)}$—23. Connecting episode.		49—57. 2nd subject in tonic key. E.
24 — 32$^{(1)}$. 2nd subject in C major. B.		57. Coda.

THIRD MOVEMENT.—"MENUETTO AND TRIO." TERNARY FORM.

Menuetto. Key of F minor. A.   Trio. Key of F major. E.

1ST PART.	2ND PART.	3RD PART.
1 — 15$^{(1)}$. 1st subject in F minor (tonic), ending in A♭ major. B.	1—11$^{(2)}$. 1st subject in F major, ending in C major. F.	Menuetto. Da Capo.
Double bar and repeat.	*Double bar and repeat.*	
16 — 30$^{(2)}$. Development. C.	12$^{(3)}$—27. Development. G.	
30$^{(3)}$—42$^{(1)}$. 1st subject beginning and ending in tonic key. D.	28 — 35. 1st subject beginning and ending in tonic key. H.	
Double bar and repeat.	*Double bar and repeat.*	

FOURTH MOVEMENT.—"PRESTISSIMO," KEY OF F MINOR. SONATA FORM. A.

ENUNCIATION.	DEVELOPMENT.	RECAPITULATION.
1 — 10 . 1st subject in F minor (tonic). B.	60—141$^{(2)}$. F.	141 — 149$^{(2)}$. 1st subject in original key. G.
10$^{(3)}$—23$^{(1)}$. Connecting episode. C.		149$^{(3)}$—164$^{(1)}$. Connecting episode. H.
23$^{(1)}$—51$^{(1)}$. 2nd subject in C minor. D.		164$^{(2)}$—192$^{(3)}$. 2nd subject in tonic key. J.
51 — 57. Coda. E.		192. Coda. K.
Double bar and repeat.		

In numbering the bars, each portion of a bar, either at the commencement or in the course of a movement, has been reckoned as one bar; the small figures in brackets denote the beat of the bar to which reference is made.

* Agnes Zimmermann's Edition of Beethoven's Sonatas (Novello) is referred to in this Analysis.

FIRST MOVEMENT.

A. The 1st subject ends at bar 9 on a half-close. It is written in 2-bar rhythm.

B. The connecting episode is principally based upon the 2nd and 3rd bars of the first subject.

C. The 2nd subject begins with the chord of the dominant minor 9th.

D. The Coda principally confirms the cadence in A♭ major.

E. The development refers to both subjects. The 1st subject, which was originally in 2-bar rhythm, occurs here, bars 50-56, in 3-bar rhythm. A pedal point of some length, bars 83-96, leads to the recapitulation.

F. The connecting episode is slightly altered; the beginning of it is transposed into the tonic key.

G. The Coda very much resembles that in the enunciation, transposed into the tonic key and slightly elongated.

SECOND MOVEMENT.

A. The 1st subject ends with a full close on the tonic. It is adapted from an early Pianoforte Quartet.[*]

B. The latter part of the 2nd subject is developed from bars 2 and 3 of the 1st subject.

C. There is no development—bar 32 modulates back to tonic key.

D. The 1st subject re-appears considerably varied, although the harmony remains almost unaltered.

E. The 2nd subject is transposed to tonic key, slightly varied.

Alternative Scheme: Ternary Form, Part I., bars 1-17; Part II., 17-32; Part III., 33-48; Coda, 48 to the end.

THIRD MOVEMENT.

A. The "Menuetto" is in Simple Binary form.

B. The 1st subject commences in F minor with a 4-bar phrase, which is repeated, bars $5^{(3)}$-$9^{(2)}$, in the relative major; it ends with another 4-bar phrase, bars $9^{(3)}$-$13^{(1)}$. The right hand parts of bars $7^{(3)}$-$9^{(3)}$ are inverted, bars $9^{(3)}$-$11^{(2)}$. Bars $11^{(3)}$-$13^{(1)}$ are repeated.

C. The development refers to the 1st subject.

D. The 1st subject re-appears, varied and shortened, and altered so as to end in tonic key.

E. The Trio is in Simple Binary form.

F. The Trio contains many instances of inverting the parts. Compare bars 6-8 (in the bass) with 2-4 (in the treble).

G. The 1st subject is referred to in the development; the parts are again inverted. Compare bars 17-19 with bars 13-15.

H. The 1st subject re-appears slightly shortened, and altered so as to end in the tonic key instead of in dominant key as before.

FOURTH MOVEMENT.

A. The long episode in the "development" has caused this movement to be sometimes described as being in Rondo form, but if it were in Rondo form, the Enunciation would have ended in tonic key with a return of the 1st subject.

B. The first part of bar 1 is introductory. The rhythm of the first subject commences upon the 3rd beat of the bar. The 1st subject ends upon the dominant chord.

C. The connecting episode commences in tonic key with the 2nd part of the 1st subject, followed by the 1st part of the same subject in the key of G (dominant of the 2nd subject), 5 bars on the dominant 7th of the key of C minor lead into the 2nd subject.

D. The 2nd subject, instead of being in the relative major key, is in the dominant minor; it contains two distinct themes, bars 23-35 and 35-51, both ending with a full close.

E. The Coda is based upon the first subject.

F. The development begins, after 2 introductory bars, with an episode in A♭ major, bars 62-112, the real "working-out" being between bars 112-141.

G. The 1st subject re-appears unaltered.

H. The connecting episode is for the most part exactly like that in the "Enunciation," transposed so as to lead into the key of the tonic.

J. The 2nd subject re-appears slightly varied, and transposed to tonic key.

K. The Coda consists entirely of a varied repetition of the commencement of the 1st subject.

[*] Dictionary of Music (Grove).

SONATA No. 2.

Op. 2, No. 2.

FIRST MOVEMENT.—"ALLEGRO VIVACE," KEY OF A MAJOR. SONATA FORM.

ENUNCIATION.	DEVELOPMENT.	RECAPITULATION.
$1 - 33^{(1)}$. 1st subject in A major (tonic). A.		$230^{(6)} - 257^{(1)}$. 1st subject in original key. F.
$33 - 59^{(9)}$. Connecting episode. B.	$127^{(4)}\text{-}229$. E.	$257 - 283^{(1)}$. Connecting episode. G.
$59^{(4)}\text{--}93^{(1)}$. 2nd subject in E minor and E major. C.		$283^{(6)} - 317^{(1)}$. 2nd subject in A minor, ending in A major. H.
$93 - 117$. Coda. D.		317. Coda. J.
Double bar and repeat. E.		Double bar and repeat from bar 127. K.

SECOND MOVEMENT.—"LARGO APPASSIONATA," KEY OF D MAJOR. TERNARY FORM.

1ST PART.	2ND PART.	3RD PART.
$1\text{-}19^{(2)}$. 1st subject in D major (tonic). A.	$19^{(9)}\text{-}32^{(11)}$. 2nd subject commencing in B minor, ending in tonic key. B.	$32\text{-}50^{(1)}$. 1st subject (varied) in original key. C.
		50. Coda. D.

THIRD MOVEMENT.—"SCHERZO AND TRIO." TERNARY FORM.

Scherzo. Key of A major. A.	Trio. Key of A minor. E.	
1ST PART.	**2ND PART.**	**3RD PART.**
$1 - 9^{(2)}$. 1st subject in A major (tonic).	$1 - 9$. 1st subject in A minor (tonic), ending in E minor.	Scherzo.
Double bar and repeat. B.	*Double bar and repeat.*	Da Capo.
$10 - 33$. Development. C.	$10\text{--}19^{(1)}$. Development. F.	
$34^{(6)} - 42^{(7)}$. Repetition of 1st subject.	$19\text{--}26$. 1st subject in original key, ending in A minor (tonic). G.	
$42^{(7)} - 46$. Coda. D.	*Double bar and repeat.*	
Double bar and repeat.		

FOURTH MOVEMENT.—"GRAZIOSO," KEY OF A MAJOR. RONDO FORM.

1ST PART.	2ND PART.	3RD PART.
$1 - 16^{(6)}$. 1st subject in A major (tonic). A.	$57\text{-}101^{(1)}$. 3rd subject in A minor. E.	$101 - 116^{(6)}$. 1st subject (varied) in original key. F.
$16^{(6)} - 26^{(1)}$. Episode. B.		$116^{(6)} - 124^{(1)}$. Episode. F.
$26 - 40$. 2nd subject in E major. C.		$125 - 136^{(11)}$. 2nd subject in A major (tonic). G.
$41 - 56^{(6)}$. 1st subject (varied) in original key. D.		$136 - 149^{(1)}$. 1st subject (varied) in original key. H.
		149. Coda. J.

In numbering the bars, each portion of a bar, either at the commencement or in the course of a movement, has been reckoned as one bar; the small figures in brackets denote the beat of the bar to which reference is made.

FIRST MOVEMENT.

A. The 1st subject, with the exception of a modulation to the dominant, bars 17-21, is entirely in the tonic key, ending with a full close, bar 33.

B. The connecting episode begins in tonic key with a passage of 2 bars in the bass, which is immediately repeated (a twelfth higher) in the treble. The same passage then occurs in the bass (a third higher than it originally did), and is followed by a modulation through the dominant major key to that of the dominant minor, in which key the connecting episode ends, bar 59.

C. The 2nd subject begins with a 4-bar phrase, $59^{(4)}$-63, in E minor, ending in G major, which is immediately repeated in G major ending in B♭ major, bars $63^{(4)}$-$67^{(1)}$; and in B♭ major, ending in D major, bars $67^{(4)}$-$71^{(1)}$; it eventually modulates to E major, in which key it closes with a 4-bar phrase, 85-88, repeated (bars 85-86 being inverted), bars 89-92.

D. The Coda is formed from previous material.

E. The development is preluded by the repetition of the last three chords of the Coda, transposed into E minor (bars 123-125). It principally refers to fragments of the 1st subject (bars 5-9); the 2nd subject is entirely ignored.

F. The 1st subject re-appears shortened and altered. Instead of the passage, bars $21^{(4)}$-$33^{(1)}$, there is a repetition of the 2-bar phrase, bars $247^{(4)}$-249, extended to 3 bars, first in D major, $250^{(4)}$-253, and then in A major (tonic), bars $254^{(4)}$-$257^{(1)}$, bringing the 1st subject to a close.

G. The connecting episode is altered so as to end in the key of the tonic minor.

H. The 2nd subject re-appears transposed to begin in tonic minor and end in tonic major; it is only very slightly altered. Compare bars 87-88 = 91-92 with bars 311-312 = 315-316.

J. The Coda, transposed into tonic key, is altered in the bass, bars 325-326.

∨ K. Repetitions of the development and recapitulation are unusual, although they will be found in Op. 10, No. 2, 1st and 3rd movements; Op. 57, 3rd movement; Op. 78, 1st movement; and Op. 79, 1st movement.

SECOND MOVEMENT.

A. The first subject begins with two 4-bar phrases, the latter ending in D major, followed by a 4-bar phrase in A major, which, at bar 12, modulates back to D major. The first two 4-bar phrases then appear compressed into one phrase of 7 bars, 13-$19^{(1)}$.

B. The 2nd subject commences in B minor, modulating to F sharp minor, bar 23, in which key the three first bars are repeated in a varied form, succeeded, at bar 26, by another variation of the same material in G major, which ends in D major, bar $32^{(1)}$, overlapping the entry of the 1st subject.

C. The first subject re-appears unaltered excepting that the parts in bars $8^{(4)}$-11 are inverted.

D. The Coda begins with a development of the figure taken from the 1st subject, bars 9-10. At bar 58 there is a reminiscence of the 1st subject in D minor, and at bar 68 the whole of the first two phrases re-appear considerably varied, ending with full close in tonic key, bar 75, which is repeated in varied form to the end of the movement.

THIRD MOVEMENT.

A. The Scherzo is in Simple Binary form.

B. The 1st subject consists of two 4-bar phrases, the first ending in the dominant, the second in the tonic key.

C. The development ends at bar 21 where an episode appears in G♯ minor, after which a passage consisting of a sequence of dominant sevenths leads back to the tonic key.

D. The short Coda is founded upon the 1st subject.

E. The Trio is in Simple Binary form.

F. The development commences in C major, modulates to D minor, and then back to A minor. The rhythm of it is identical with that of Part I.

G. The 1st subject re-appears varied and altered so as to end in A minor, instead of E minor as before.

FOURTH MOVEMENT.

A. The 1st subject begins with a 4-bar phrase ending on half-close on dominant, followed by another 4-bar phrase ending with full close on dominant. A 4-bar phrase on dominant pedal point is succeeded by another one of the same length similar to bars 1-4, but altered to end in tonic key.

B. The episode begins with a new subject in the tonic key, modulating to the dominant, in which it ends, bar 26.

C. The 2nd subject commences with a phrase in E major, bars $26^{(4)}$-$28^{(4)}$, which is immediately repeated (varied) twice. A sequential passage leads to an inverted dominant pedal point preparatory to the second entry of 1st subject in tonic key.

D. The 1st subject is varied at each repetition.

E. The 3rd subject is based almost entirely upon the figure in bar 57. It commences in A minor and modulates to C, in which key there is a full close, bar 66 (double bar and repeat from bar 57), this is followed by a passage (in imitation, bars 68-72) ending in E major, bar 75. Bars 57-$61^{(1)}$ are then repeated (with slight variation), bars 76-$80^{(1)}$. Bars 68-80 then recur, the last two bars, however, 79-80, are altered, bars 92-93, to end on the dominant. Bars 93-100 form a passage leading to part 3.

F. The original episode is slightly altered and shortened.

G. The 2nd subject re-appears transposed into the tonic key, it is also slightly altered. Compare bars 27 and 29 with 125 and 127. It ends with full close in the tonic.

H. The 1st subject re-appears *considerably* varied. At bar 141-142 there is a modulation to F major. By enharmonic change, bars $145^{(4)}$-$146^{(1)}$ modulate back to tonic key.

J. The Coda consists of modulating reminiscences of 1st and 3rd subjects.

SONATA No. 3.

Op. 2, No. 3.

FIRST MOVEMENT.—"ALLEGRO CON BRIO," KEY OF C MAJOR. SONATA FORM.

ENUNCIATION.	DEVELOPMENT.	RECAPITULATION.
1 — 13$^{(1)}$. 1st subject in C major (tonic). A.	91$^{(8)}$—140$^{(1)}$. E.	140 — 147. 1st subject in original key. F.
13 — 26. Connecting episode. B.		148 — 161. Connecting episode. G.
27 — 77$^{(1)}$. 2nd subject in G minor and G major. C.		162 — 212$^{(1)}$. 2nd subject in C minor and C major.
77$^{(8)}$—9c. Coda. D.		212$^{(8)}$. Coda. H.
Double bar and repeat.		

SECOND MOVEMENT.—"ADAGIO," KEY OF E MAJOR. MODIFIED RONDO FORM. A.

1ST PART.	2ND PART.	3RD PART.
1—11$^{(1)}$. 1st subject in E major (tonic). B.	D.	53—54. E.
11—43$^{(1)}$. 2nd subject in E minor and G major. C.		55—66. 2nd subject in E major (tonic). F.
		67—77$^{(1)}$. 1st subject (varied) in original key.
43—53$^{(1)}$. 1st subject in original key.		77. Coda. G.

THIRD MOVEMENT.—"SCHERZO AND TRIO." TERNARY FORM.

Scherzo. Key of C major. A.   Trio. Key of A minor. C.

1ST PART.	2ND PART.	3RD PART.
1 — 17$^{(1)}$. 1st subject in C major (tonic), ending in G major.	1 — 8. 1st subject in A minor (tonic), ending in E minor.	Scherzo. Da Capo.
Double bar and repeat.	*Double bar and repeat.*	43. Coda.
18$^{(8)}$—41$^{(8)}$. Development. B.	9$^{(3)}$—18$^{(1)}$. Development.	
41$^{(8)}$—57$^{(1)}$. 1st subject in original key altered so as to end in tonic key.	18 — 25. 1st subject in original key altered so as to end in A minor (tonic).	
57$^{(8)}$. Coda.	25$^{(3)}$—42. D.	
Double bar and repeat from bar 18.		

FOURTH MOVEMENT.—"ALLEGRO ASSAI," KEY OF C MAJOR. RONDO FORM.

1ST PART.	2ND PART.	3RD PART.
1 — 9$^{(8)}$. 1st subject in C major (tonic). A.	77$^{(6)}$—182$^{(1)}$. Development and (E) 3rd subject in F major.	182 — 197$^{(1)}$. 1st subject in original key. F.
9$^{(6)}$—30. Episode. B.		197$^{(8)}$—218. Episode. G.
31—64$^{(1)}$. 2nd subject in G major. C.		219 — 254$^{(1)}$. 2nd subject in C major (tonic). H.
64—70$^{(1)}$. D.		254 — 260$^{(1)}$. J.
70—77$^{(1)}$. 1st subject in original key.		260. 1st subject (abbreviated) in original key. K.

In numbering the bars, each portion of a bar, either at the commencement or in the course of a movement, has been reckoned as one bar; the small figures in brackets denote the beat of the bar to which reference is made.

FIRST MOVEMENT.

A. The 1st subject is constructed almost entirely upon the 1st bar rhythm, it ends at bar 8[III]; bars 9-13 being a varied and prolonged repetition of bars 5-8[III].

B. The connecting episode is formed of new material; it ends upon the dominant, which is unusual.

C. The second subject (which is adapted from an early Pianoforte Quartet*) begins with a 2-bar phrase, succeeded by a 4-bar phrase. It is in 2 parts, G minor (dominant minor), bars 27-45, and G major (dominant major), bars 47-77. The 2nd subject recurs in C minor (tonic minor) and C major (tonic major), bars 162-182. See also Op. 2, No. 2, 1st movement. Alternative scheme: Connecting episode, bars 13-46; second subject, bars 47-77.

D. The Coda commences with a short subject, which is afterwards introduced at the beginning of the development.

E. The development begins with the subject referred to in letter D, followed by a brilliant passage in arpeggios. At bars 103-104 there is an enharmonic modulation leading to the 1st subject in D major, bar 110. It closes upon dominant pedal point.

F. The 1st subject re-appears shortened; the varied repetition of bars 5-8[III] being omitted.

G. The brilliant 8 bars at the commencement of the connecting episode are omitted, and a development of the last 2 bars of the 1st subject is substituted. The last part is unaltered.

H. The Coda begins with the same subject as in the enunciation, followed by a passage in arpeggios leading to a cadenza, after which the movement ends with a reference to the 1st subject.

SECOND MOVEMENT.

A. This movement is in modified Rondo form.

B. The 1st subject ends at bar 8[III]; bars 8[(4)] 11[(1)] being a varied prolongation of bars 6[(4)]-8[III].

C. The 2nd subject instead of being in B major is principally in E minor and G major. It may be divided into 2 parts:— the 1st part, bars 11-19[(1)], beginning in E minor and ending in G major; the 2nd part, bars 19-25[(1)], beginning and ending in G major. Bars 26-37[(1)] consist of a development of part 1, and bars 37-43[(1)] of a varied repetition of part 2.

D. There is no second part of any kind to this movement.

E. These 2 bars in C major are suggestive of the 1st subject. As the 3rd subject is omitted, another repetition of 1st subject is unnecessary here.

F. The 2nd subject re-appears considerably curtailed. It commences with a passage, bars 55-58, suggestive of the 1st part, modulating to E major, in which key the 2nd part occurs. Bars 26-42 are omitted.

G. The Coda refers to the 1st subject.

THIRD MOVEMENT.

A. The Scherzo is in Simple Binary form.

B. At bar 30 of the development a figure is introduced, which appears in the Coda.

C. The Trio is in Simple Binary form.

D. Instead of the usual double bar and repeat, the repetition is written out in full, with slight alterations at the end.

FOURTH MOVEMENT.

A. The 1st subject consists of two sections of equal length (4 bars), both constructed upon the same rhythm, forming a sentence of 8 bars.

B. The episode is formed upon dominant pedal point, followed by a varied repetition of the 1st section of the 1st subject, and some development of bars 4-5.

C. The 2nd subject commences in G major, it modulates to G minor, bar 44, and ends bar 64, after 8 bars upon dominant pedal point. Alternative scheme: 2nd subject, bars 31-40; connecting passage, bars 40-70.

D. Bars 64-69 form a passage leading to the second entry of the 1st subject.

E. The development commences with a reference to the 1st subject followed by a passage leading to the 3rd subject, which enters in F major, bar 104, in 2-bar rhythm. At bar 144 there is a development of the first two phrases of the 3rd subject ending upon dominant pedal point, which continues for 13 bars, preparatory to the 3rd entry of the 1st subject.

F. The 1st subject re-appears with a varied elongation.

G. The last 5 bars of the episode are altered to end in G instead of D. Compare bars 25-29 with 213-217.

H. The 1st part of the 2nd subject re-appears transposed into tonic key and elongated by 2 bars. The 2nd part remains in the same key as before, slightly varied.

J. Bars 254-259 form a passage preparatory to the 4th entry of the 1st subject.

K. The re-appearance of the 1st subject takes the form of a Coda. The 1st subject does not appear in its entirety. Note the inverted pedal point, bars 260-265, and the prolonged interrupted cadence where the chord of the dominant seventh (by raising the fifth D to D♯) resolves into the chord of A major, bar 299.

* Dictionary of Music (Grove).

SONATA No. 4.

Op. 7.

FIRST MOVEMENT.—"Allegro Molto e con Brio," key of E♭ major. Sonata Form.

Enunciation.	Development.	Recapitulation.
1 — 17[(1)]. 1st subject in E♭ major (tonic). A.		189 — 201[(1)]. 1st subject in original key. F.
17 — 41[(1)]. Connecting episode. B.	137—188. E.	201 — 220. Connecting episode. G.
41 — 127[(1)]. 2nd subject in B♭ major. C.		221 — 307[(1)]. 2nd subject in E♭ major (tonic).
127[(8)]—136. Coda. D.		307[(8)]. Coda. H.
Double bar and repeat.		

SECOND MOVEMENT.—"Largo con gran espressione," key of C major. Ternary Form. A.

1st Part.	2nd Part.	3rd Part.
1—24. 1st subject in C major (tonic). B.	29—51[(1)]. E.	51—74[(1)]. 1st subject (varied) in original key.
24. C.		74—84[(1)]. 2nd subject (varied) in C major (tonic). F.
25—28. 2nd subject beginning in A♭ major. D.		84. Coda. G.

THIRD MOVEMENT.—"Allegro" and "Minore." Ternary Form. A.

Allegro. Key of E♭ major. B.   Minore. Key of E♭ minor. K.

1st Part.			2nd Part.	3rd Part
Enunciation.	Development.	Recapitulation.	1—17[(1)]. 1st subject in E♭ minor (tonic), ending in B♭ major. L.	
1 — 8. 1st subject in E♭ major (tonic). C.		43 — 50. 1st subject in original key.		
9 — 14. Connecting episode. D.	25·43[(1)]. F.	51 — 71[(1)]. Connecting episode. G.	*Double bar and repeat.*	
15[(8)]—24. 2nd subject in B♭ major. E.		71[(3)]—86. 2nd subject (varied) in E♭ major (tonic). H.	18—31. Development. M.	
Double bar and repeat.		87. Coda. J.	31—45[(1)]. 1st subject in original key. N.	Da Capo.
		Double bar and repeat from bar 25.	45. Coda. O.	"Allegro."

FOURTH MOVEMENT.—"Poco Allegretto e Grazioso," key of E♭ major. Rondo Form.

1st Part.	2nd Part.	3rd Part.
1 — 17. 1st subject in E♭ major (tonic). A.		97[(3)]—113. 1st subject (varied) in original key.
17[(8)]—37[(1)]. Episode. B.	65—91. 3rd subject in C minor. F.	113[(8)]—133[(1)]. Episode. G.
37[(8)]—49. 2nd subject in B♭ major. C.		133[(8)]—145. 2nd subject in E♭ major (tonic). H.
49 — 51. Connecting passage modulating to tonic key. D.	91—97[(2)]. Connecting passage.	146[(8)]—170[(1)]. 1st subject in original key. J.
51[(8)]—63. 1st subject in original key. E.		170. Coda. K.

In numbering the bars, each portion of a bar, either at the commencement or in the course of a movement has been reckoned as one bar; the small figures in brackets denote the beat of the bar to which reference is made.

FIRST MOVEMENT.

A. The 1st subject is constructed on two distinct figures, bars 1-2 and 5-6. It ends with full close on the tonic, bar 17[1].

B. The connecting episode commences with a 4-bar passage, bars 17-20, which appears inverted, bars 21-24. It ends on pedal point.

C. The 2nd subject may be divided into 4 parts, all in the key of the dominant :—1st part, bars 41-59; 2nd part, bars 59-93; 3rd part, bars 93-111; 4th part, bars 111-127[1]. The last is entirely constructed on dominant pedal point. Alternative scheme : Connecting episode, bars 17-59; 2nd subject, 59-127.

D. The Coda consists of two bars (127[1]-128) repeated (varied) 3 times in succession, simply confirming the perfect cadence.

E. The development contains references to the 1st subject, the connecting episode figure, bars 141-163, and also to some material found in the Coda.

F. The 1st subject re-appears shortened, the concluding 4 bars being omitted.

G. The connecting episode re-appears considerably altered ; it branches off from what was before the concluding phrase of the 1st subject ; at bar 215 it reverts to the original, the last six bars of which (with slight inversion of parts) appear transposed into B♭ major.

H. The Coda only resembles the original in the first 6 bars; it then refers to both the 1st and 2nd subjects, and to the first Coda.

SECOND MOVEMENT.

A. The form of this movement somewhat resembles Sonata Form. The key of C is an unusual one for a 2nd movement when the 1st movement is in the key of E♭.

B. The 1st subject consists of an 8-bar sentence ending in C major, followed by a 4-bar sentence in G major, after which there is a varied and extended repetition of bars 1-8.

C. The transition from 1st subject to 2nd subject is affected by the passage in bar 24.

D. The 2nd subject, instead of being in G major, appears in A♭ major ; it only consists of a phrase of 4 bars.

E. The development commences with a 4-bar phrase in F minor based on 2nd subject, bars 29-32. At bar 33 a great portion of the 2nd subject appears in D♭ major. Bars 37-50 constitute a passage, leading back to tonic key, which contains some development of the 1st subject.

F. The 2nd subject re-appears transposed into tonic key, varied and extended.

G. The Coda chiefly refers to previous material ; the last 4 bars consist of a varied repetition of bars 1-4 differently harmonised.

THIRD MOVEMENT.

A. These movements really constitute a Minuet and Trio, though not so designated.

B. The Allegro (Minuet) is in Sonata form.

C. The 1st subject ends with half-close on the dominant.

D. The connecting episode consists of bars 1-4 altered at the end, by the insertion of a cadence in C minor, which is repeated in B♭ major (dominant).

E. The 2nd subject commences with a figure taken from bars 3[1]-4[1], which is repeated 4 times.

F. The development begins with a canonical reference to the 1st subject.

G. The connecting episode re-appears extended ; it commences with the same material as before, transposed into E♭ minor, followed by a passage in C♭ major; it ends on the chord of the augmented 6th (key of E♭ major), followed by 2 bars on the dominant.

H. The 2nd subject re-appears varied and extended and transposed into tonic key.

J. The Coda is constructed on pedal point in the bass.

K. The " Minore " (Trio) is in Simple Binary form.

L. This movement is in triplets throughout.

M. The development begins in B♭ minor and ends in E♭ minor.

N. The 1st subject re-appears altered so as to end in tonic key.

O. The Coda is built upon tonic pedal point in the bass.

FOURTH MOVEMENT.

A. The 1st subject consists of a sentence of 8 bars, ending with full close on tonic, repeated varied, bars 9[1]-17[1].

B. The episode begins with a phrase borrowed from the 1st subject (bars 9-10). It modulates to the dominant, in which key a new figure is introduced in the bass (bars 25-26), the latter part of which is repeated 12 times in the succeeding 8 bars. It ends with full close in B♭ major.

C. The 2nd subject consists of a sentence of 8 bars (37[1]-45[1]), beginning in C minor and ending in B♭ major. Bars 45-48 are a varied repetition of bars 43-44.

D. After the 2nd subject there follows a passage leading to tonic key, bars 49-51.

(9)

E. The 1st subject re-appears curtailed. After arriving at the note B♭, bar 63, which corresponds to the pause note in the original (bar 13), it is cut short by the note B♮, bar 64, leading into the key of C minor.

F. The 3rd subject is divided into two parts, both founded upon the same figures, and both repeated It ends, bar 91, after which there is a passage leading into the third appearance of the 1st subject.

G. The episode re-appears slightly altered and transposed so as to end in tonic key.

H. The 2nd subject re-appears transposed into tonic key.

J. The 1st subject re-appears varied. After arriving at the pause referred to at D, it proceeds in the key of E major for a few bars, ending ultimately in tonic key.

K. The Coda is constructed on similar figures to the 3rd subject.

SONATA No. 5.

Op. 10, No. 1.

FIRST MOVEMENT.—"Allegro molto e con brio," key of C minor. Sonata Form.

ENUNCIATION.	DEVELOPMENT.	RECAPITULATION.
1—31. 1st subject in C minor (tonic). A.	106—168[1]. E.	168—190. 1st subject in original key. F.
32—56[1]. Connecting episode. B.		191—215[1]. Connecting episode. G.
56—94[1]. 2nd subject in E♭ major. C.		215—233[1]. 2nd subject in F major. H.
94-105. Coda. D.		233—271[1]. And in C minor (tonic).
Double bar and repeat.		271. Coda. J. L.

SECOND MOVEMENT.—"Adagio Molto," key of A♭ major. Modified Sonata Form.

ENUNCIATION.	DEVELOPMENT.	RECAPITULATION.
1—16. 1st subject in A♭ major (tonic). A.	45. D.	46—61. 1st subject (varied) in original key.
17—24[1]. Connecting episode. B.		62—71[1]. Connecting episode. E.
24—44 2nd subject in E♭ major. C.		71—91. 2nd subject in A♭ major (tonic).
		91. Coda. F.

THIRD MOVEMENT.—"Prestissimo," "Finale," key of C minor. Sonata Form.

ENUNCIATION.	DEVELOPMENT.	RECAPITULATION.
1—9[1]. 1st subject in C minor (tonic). A.	48—59[1]. E.	59[1]—67[1]. 1st subject in original key.
9[1]—17[1]. Connecting episode. B.		67[1]—75[1]. Connecting episode. F.
17[1]—29[1]. 2nd subject in E♭ major. C.		75[1]—87[1]. 2nd subject in C major. G.
29—47. Coda. D.		87. Coda. H.
Double bar and repeat.		

In numbering the bars, each portion of a bar, either at the commencement or in the course of a movement, has been reckoned as one bar; the small figures in brackets denote the beat of the bar to which reference is made.

FIRST MOVEMENT.

A. The 1st subject, which consists of nothing but tonic and dominant harmony of C minor, begins with two 4-bar phrases, which are condensed to 2-bar phrases at bars 22-27.

B. The connecting episode (with one introductory bar on E♭) begins with a melodious phrase, which occurs 3 times, constructed upon the tonic and dominant harmony of the keys of A♭ major, F minor, and D♭ major respectively. After 4 bars of modulation there is a pedal point in the bass upon B♭ for 8 bars. Bar 45 contains three different forms of the chord of the augmented 6th (French, German, and Italian).

C. The 2nd subject is in 4-bar rhythm. After the chord of the $\frac{6}{4}$, bar 86, there is a reminiscence of the 1st subject. It ends with full close in E♭ major.

D. The Coda is formed upon the closing part of the connecting episode.

E. The development commences with a part of the 1st subject in C major. At bar 118 the 2nd subject is developed for 8 bars in F minor, repeated in B♭ minor. These 16 bars contain nothing but tonic and dominant harmonies of the respective keys. Bars 136-167 form a passage taken from the connecting episode, leading to the re-entry of the 1st subject.

F. The 1st subject re-appears shortened, bars 22-30 being omitted.

G. The 1st phrase of the original connecting episode is transposed from A♭ major to G♭ major, its first repetition from F minor to G♭ major, and its 2nd repetition from D♭ major to E♭ minor; the concluding part (pedal point) being upon the note C instead of B♭.

H. The 2nd subject re-appears shortened, and transposed into F major instead of into the tonic key C minor. At bar 233, however, the whole subject recurs in the latter key.

J. The Coda is slightly altered and transposed into the tonic key.

L. The subdominant chord only occurs once throughout the whole of the principal subjects and Codas —viz., in bar 72, subdominant of E♭ (repeated bar 80, and of course in the Recapitulation).

SECOND MOVEMENT.

A. The 1st subject begins with two phrases of 2 bars each, followed by a phrase of 4 bars ending with half-close on the dominant. These phrases are then repeated (varied), ending with full close in the tonic key.

B. The connecting episode commences with a 2-bar phrase in B♭ minor, repeated in A♭ major; an imitation of it is used to modulate to E♭ major.

C. The 2nd subject begins with a 4-bar phrase, 24-27, repeated varied, bars 28-31[a]. This is followed by another phrase, bars 31-35, which is also repeated (varied), ending with full close in E♭ major, bar 44.

D. There is no development in this movement, its place being taken by simply an arpeggio chord of the dominant 7th, bar 45.

E. The connecting episode re-appears altered after the first 3 bars so as to end in tonic key instead of in dominant. It is also elongated. Compare bars 65-70 with 20-23.

F. The Coda is formed upon the 1st subject; it contains syncopation in every bar but the last two.

THIRD MOVEMENT.

A. The whole of the 1st subject is founded upon the first 6 notes.

B. The connecting episode begins with reference to the 1st subject upon tonic pedal point for 4 bars. After some florid passages it closes with dominant chord (G), which is an unusual one to precede the key of E♭ major.

C. The 2nd subject ends at bar 25[a], the following bars being a short development of the last two bars.

D. The Coda commences with a variation of the 1st subject in the key of the relative major (in the bass, bars 29-30, then in the treble, bar 31). The following 3 bars (32-34) are immediately repeated, with slight variation. Bars 38-40 are treated in the same way. The Coda closes on pedal point in E♭ major.

E. The development is of slight dimensions and only refers to the 1st subject.

F. The connecting episode is slightly varied and is not transposed.

G. The 2nd subject re-appears in C major instead of C minor; it, however, ends in C minor.

H. The Coda is transposed into tonic key to bar 103, where there are added 5 bars in D♭ major, ending (on pause) on dominant 7th, followed by the first 5 bars of the 2nd subject, still in the same key (D♭), and again ending on dominant 7th. After an enharmonic modulation (by chord of diminished 7th) to the key of the tonic, it closes with a tonic pedal point, upon which are alternately the first 6 notes of the 2nd subject and the first 6 notes of the 1st subject.

SONATA No. 6.

Op. 10, No. 2.

FIRST MOVEMENT.—"Allegro," key of F major. Sonata Form.

Enunciation.	Development.	Recapitulation.
1 — 13(1). 1st subject in F major (tonic). A.	69 — 79.	120 — 132. 1st subject in D major. F.
13(1)—19(1). Connecting episode. B.	79 — 97. Episode. E.	133 — 148(1). Connecting episode. G.
19(1)—56(1). 2nd subject in C major. C.	97—119.	148(1)—193(1). 2nd subject in F major. H.
56(3)—67. Coda. D.		193(3). Coda. J.
Double bar and repeat.		Double bar and repeat from bar 69. K.

SECOND MOVEMENT.—"Allegretto." A. Ternary Form.

Menuetto. Key of F minor. B.   Trio. Key of D♭ major. C.

1st Part.	2nd Part.	3rd Part.
1 — 9. 1st subject in F minor (tonic) ending in A♭ major.	41 — 57(1). 1st subject in D♭ major (tonic) ending in A♭ major.	F.
Double bar and repeat.	57(3)—73(1). *Repeated (varied).*	Repetition of 1st Part
10—18. Sequential passage.	73(1)—82. Development. D.	(Menuetto), bar 128 to end.
18—32. 1st subject in original key so altered as to end in F minor (tonic).	82 — 96. 1st subject in original key altered so as to end in D♭ major (tonic).	
32—40. Coda.	97—121. *Repeat from bar 73.*	
Double bar and repeat from bar 10.	122—127. Connecting passage. E.	

THIRD MOVEMENT.—"Presto," key of F major. Sonata Form.

Enunciation.	Development.	Recapitulation.
1——9(3). 1st subject in F major (tonic). A.	34—87. D.	88(1)— 96. 1st subject in original key. E.
9(1)—24(1). Connecting episode.		96(2)—127(1). Connecting episode. F.
24 — 33. 2nd subject in C major.		127. 2nd subject in F major (tonic). G.
Double bar and repeat.		Double bar and repeat from bar 34. H.

In numbering the bars, each portion of a bar, either at the commencement or in the course of a movement, has been reckoned as one bar; the small figures in brackets denote the beat of the bar to which reference is made.

FIRST MOVEMENT.

A. The 1st subject consists of 12 bars divided into 3 sections of 4 bars each.

B. The connecting episode begins with the first 2 bars of the 1st subject, which are repeated with the addition of D$\sharp$ (enharmonic modulation E$\flat$-D$\sharp$) to the harmony, producing the chord of the augmented 6th resolving on dominant of A (this resolution takes place 3 times), an unusual chord to precede the key of C major. (*See* bars 17-18, Third movement, Sonata, No. 5.)

C. The 2nd subject commences, in C major, with three 4-bar phrases, the last modulating to G major, in which key there is a passage, bars 31-37[1], consisting of tonic and dominant harmony, leading to a new phrase of 4 bars which is repeated (varied) in C minor. A chord of the diminished 7th on F$\sharp$, bar 47, is followed by another new 4-bar phrase, bars 48-51, after which 2 bars of the triplet figure (bar 2) lead to a full close in C major. Some writers consider that the 2nd subject consists only of bars 19-27.

D. The Coda consists of a 4-bar phrase repeated with slight variations and elongations. At bar 64 there is a curious harmonic combination of the chord of the diminished 7th (supertonic root) on inverted dominant pedal.

E. The last 2 bars of the Coda are developed, bars 69-79, followed by an episode beginning in D minor. Bars 85-89 resemble bars 79-83 transposed into G minor; the same 4 bars are tranposed into B$\flat$ major, bars 93-97. A development of the last 2 bars of the Coda in B$\flat$ major and B$\flat$ minor, bar 97, and some episodal modulation, lead to the chord of the dominant of the key of D.

F. The 1st subject is in D major instead of being in tonic key.

G. The connecting episode re-appears with some modulating bars based upon the 1st subject, followed by the 2nd and 3rd sections of the 1st subject in the key of the tonic, bars 140-148.

H. A sequential passage formed upon the first phrase of the 2nd subject, bars 157-166, does not appear in the enunciation.

J. The final cadence of the Coda is repeated.

K. The repetition of development and recapitulation is unusual.

SECOND MOVEMENT.

A. Menuetto and Trio, though designated " Allegretto."

B. The 1st part (Menuetto) is in Simple Binary form.

C. The 2nd part (Trio) is in Simple Binary form.

D. The development is very short; it is based on the 1st subject.

E. After the 2nd part there is a passage of 6 bars, 122-127, leading back to the key of the tonic.

F. The 1st part is repeated considerably varied. The bass of the episode, bars 144-151, is written in quavers, and on the recurrence of the 1st subject syncopation is freely employed.

THIRD MOVEMENT.

A. The 1st subject, consisting of 4 bars, leads off (in the bass) in fugal style answered at the 8th, bar 5 (in the treble).

B. The connecting episode, which is in the key of the dominant, begins with the first subject, upon which it is founded.

C. The 2nd subject is written upon a pedal point.

D. The development refers to the 1st subject principally. Note the appearance of the 2nd subject (varied) in the key of D major, bar 71. The development ends on dominant 7th, bar 87, succeeded by a scale passage which overlaps the entry of the 1st subject.

E. The 1st subject re-appears accompanied by a scale passage.

F. The connecting episode re-appears beginning with a passage of 4 bars (96[m]-100) in G minor. This passage is repeated in G minor and B$\flat$ major, bars 100-108. A brilliant variation of the 1st subject, beginning in B$\flat$ minor and ending on the dominant chord, leads to the re-entry of the 2nd subject in the tonic key.

G. The 2nd subject re-appears extended, forming a short Coda.

H. The repetition of development and recapitulation is unusual.

SONATA No. 7.

Op. 10, No. 3.

FIRST MOVEMENT.—"Presto," key of D major. Sonata Form.

Enunciation.	Development.	Recapitulation.
$1 — 11^{(1)}$. 1st subject in D major (tonic). A.		$185^{(4)}—195^{(1)}$. 1st subject in original key.
$11^{(4)}— 23^{(1)}$. Connecting episode. B.	$135—185^{(1)}$. F.	$195^{(4)}—206$. Connecting episode. G.
$23^{(4)}— 94^{(1)}$. 2nd subject in B minor and A major. C.		$206 — 276^{(1)}$. 2nd subject in E minor and D major (tonic). H.
$94^{(4)}—114^{(1)}$. Coda. D.		$276^{(4)}$. Coda. J.
$114^{(4)}—125$. E.		
Double bar and repeat.		

SECOND MOVEMENT.—"Largo e mesto," key of D minor. Ternary Form.

1st Part.	2nd Part.	3rd Part.
$1 — 9^{(1)}$. 1st subject in D minor (tonic). A.		$44 — 48$. 1st subject in original key. F.
$9^{(4)}—17^{(1)}$. Connecting episode. B.	$30—43$. E.	$49 — 56^{(1)}$. Connecting episode. G.
$17^{(8)}—26^{(1)}$. 2nd subject in A minor. C.		$56^{(8)}—65^{(1)}$. 2nd subject in D minor (tonic).
$26 — 29$. Coda. D.		65. Coda. H.
Double bar. No repeat.		

THIRD MOVEMENT.—"Allegro." "Menuetto and Trio." Ternary Form.

Menuetto. Key of D major. A.   Trio. Key of G major.

1st Part.	2nd Part.	3rd Part.
1—17. 1st subject in D major (tonic). B.	1—33. Subject in G major (tonic). E.	Menuetto.
Double bar and repeat.		Da Capo.
18—26. Episode. C.		
27—45. 1st subject in original key. D.	*Double bar.*	
45. Coda.		
Double bar and repeat from bar 18.		

FOURTH MOVEMENT.—"Allegro," key of D major. Rondo Form.

1st Part.	2nd Part.	3rd Part.
$1 — 10^{(1)}$. 1st subject in D major (tonic). A.	$34—56$. Episode in B♭ major. C.	$57 — 66^{(1)}$. 1st subject (varied) in original key.
$10^{(4)}—25^{(1)}$. Episode. B.		$66^{(8)}—85^{(1)}$. Episode. D.
$25^{(4)}—34^{(1)}$. 1st subject in original key.		$85^{(4)}—94^{(1)}$. 1st subject (varied) in original key.
		94. Coda. E.

In numbering the bars, each portion of a bar, either at the commencement or in the course of a movement, has been reckoned as one bar; the small figures in brackets denote the beat of the bar to which reference is made.

FIRST MOVEMENT.

A. The 1st subject begins with a 4-bar phrase ending on dominant, bar 5, followed by a 6-bar phrase which ends with full close in tonic key.

B. The connecting episode begins with a continuation of the 1st subject. Bars 17-23 are a variation and elongation of bars 1-5, ending upon the dominant of relative minor.

C. * The 2nd subject is divided into two parts, bars 23-54, 54-94. It commences with a theme in B minor, modulating to F♯ minor, A major, and E major, ending in A major; the 2nd part of the 2nd subject begins with a sentence of 8 bars in A major, partly repeated, bars 61-66, in A minor, followed by a new phrase (the bass of which is taken from the beginning of the first subject), which is developed at some length, giving place at bar 88 to a passage in A major, which brings the 2nd section to a close, bar 94.

D. The Coda consists of some new material and slight references to the 1st subject, for the most part on a pedal point.

E. Bars 114⁽⁴⁾-125 form a passage leading to the repetition of the enunciation, after which, with bars 126-134, it leads to the development.

F. The development, beginning in B♭ major, chiefly refers to the 1st subject, the rhythm of the first 5 bars of which is the basis upon which most of it is constructed: compare rhythm of bars $135^{(4)}$-$139^{(3)}$ with bars 1-$5^{(3)}$. It ends on dominant 7th, bar 185.

G. The connecting episode, after a few bars, is altered to end in E minor.

H. The 2nd subject re-appears, slightly altered and transposed; it begins in E minor and ends in the tonic key.

J. The Coda is slightly altered and transposed to end in D major.

SECOND MOVEMENT.

A. The 1st subject is of 9 bars length, the first section of 4 bars being lengthened to 5 bars; it begins and ends in tonic key.

B. The connecting episode begins in D minor and ends in C major : it consists of two sections of 4 bars each.

C. The second subject, instead of being in the relative major, is in the dominant minor key. It begins with a sentence of 4 bars, which is repeated, varied, and elongated.

D. The Coda is formed from a part of the connecting episode, bars $13^{(4)}$-$15^{(4)}$.

E. Part II. consists of an episode in F major, modulating to D minor, and ending on dominant pedal point.

F. The second section of the first subject is omitted.

G. The connecting episode re-appears altered for the first 4 bars, after which it is transposed from C major to B♭ major.

H. The Coda is entirely altered, the first 2 bars of the 1st subject appear in the bass, accompanied by a semiquaver figure in the treble, after which the bass rises chromatically from A♮ to the octave above (omitting F♯). The harmony abounds in chords of the diminished 7th. A pedal point on A (the dominant) and some slight reminiscences of the 1st subject bring the Coda to a close.

THIRD MOVEMENT.

A. The Menuetto is in Simple Binary form.

B. The 1st subject consists of a section of 8 bars, ending with half-close on the dominant, followed by another section of the same length, ending with full close in tonic key.

C. The modulating episode consists of a 3-bar subject answered (omitting the first note) at the fourth above.

D. The first subject re-appears varied and extended. The first 3 bars are accompanied by an inverted pedal point on the dominant.

E. The first 16 bars, which close on the chord of D, are repeated (bars 17 to the end) with slight alterations, finishing on the chord of the dominant 7th of D.

FOURTH MOVEMENT.

A. The 1st subject consists of a section of 4 bars ending in dominant key, followed by a section of the same length, ending with full close in tonic key.

B. This episode begins with a phrase of 2 bars in D major, which is repeated three times, modulating to A major, in which key another phrase of 4 bars occurs, which is partly repeated, ending on dominant 7th.

C. This episode in B♭ major overlaps the last chord of the 1st subject. It begins with 2 bars of introduction suggestive of the commencement of the 1st subject, followed by a phrase, bars 36-38⁽¹⁾, which is repeated in G minor and E♭ major. A passage, bars 42-46, in the latter key, ends on dominant 7th of F major; this is succeeded by some episodal modulation founded on the 1st subject and ending on dominant 7th, bar 56.

D. This episode begins like that in part 1; there is some fresh material at the end of it, based upon the rhythm of the 1st figure of the 1st subject.

E. The Coda is very original and contains many points of interest: note the rising sequence (bars 94-97), the pause on the chord of the 11th (bar 100), the first subject figure in the bass against the chromatic runs in the treble (bars 108-111), and the pedal point (bars 108 to the end).

* Some theorists consider that the 2nd subject begins at bar 54.

SONATA No. 8.

Op. 13.

1—10. A.—INTRODUCTION, "GRAVE," KEY OF C MINOR (TONIC).

FIRST MOVEMENT.—"ALLEGRO DI MOLTO E CON BRIO," KEY OF C MINOR. SONATA FORM.

ENUNCIATION.	DEVELOPMENT.	RECAPITULATION.
1 —— 9[(1)]. 1st subject in C minor (tonic). B.	125—187[(1)]. F.	187—195[(1)]. 1st subject in original key.
9 — 41[(1)]. Connecting episode. C.		195—213. Connecting episode. G.
41[(8)]—111[(1)]. 2nd subject in E♭ minor and E♭ major. D.		213—277[(1)]. 2nd subject in F minor and C minor. H.
111 — 124. Coda. E.		277. Coda. J.
Double bar and repeat.		

SECOND MOVEMENT.—"ADAGIO CANTABILE," KEY OF A♭ MAJOR. RONDO FORM. A.

1ST PART.	2ND PART.	3RD PART.
1 — 16[(8)]. 1st subject in A♭ major (tonic). B.	37—51[(1)]. Episode. E.	51—66[(1)]. 1st subject in original key. F.
16[(b)]—29[(1)]. Episode beginning in F minor. C.		66. Coda.
29 — 36[(8)]. 1st subject in original key. D.		

THIRD MOVEMENT.—"ALLEGRO," KEY OF C MINOR. RONDO FORM.

1ST PART.	2ND PART.	3RD PART.
1 — 18. 1st subject in C minor (tonic). A.	79[(8)]—108[(1)]. 3rd subject in A♭. E.	121[(8)]—129[(1)]. 1st subject in original key. G.
19 — 26[(1)]. Episode. B.	108 — 121[(1)]. F.	129 — 135[(1)]. Episode. H.
26 — 44. 2nd subject in E♭ major. C.		135 — 154[(1)]. 2nd subject in C major (tonic).
44 — 62[(1)]. D.		154[(4)]—172[(1)]. J.
62[(8)]—79[(1)]. 1st subject in original key.		172 — 183[(1)]. 1st subject in original key. K.
		183. Coda. L.

In numbering the bars, each portion of a bar, either at the commencement or in the course of a movement, has been reckoned as one bar; the small figures in brackets denote the beat of the bar to which reference is made.

FIRST MOVEMENT.

A. This is the first of the Sonatas (taking them in the order in which they appeared) with an introduction. The 1st bar phrase is the groundwork upon which the whole of the introduction is written. It is very modulatory in character, ending on the chord of the dominant minor 9th.

B. Rhythmically the 1st subject ends at the end of bar 8. The first 4 bars are constructed upon tonic pedal point.

C. The connecting episode begins with a repetition of the 1st subject ending upon the dominant, bars 9-17, followed by a passage in C minor, also ending upon the dominant, bars 17-21, repeated, bars 21-25. Three passages founded upon the 1st subject, bars 25-27 (key of G), 28-31 (key of A♭), and 32-35 (key of B♭), and 6 bars, 35-40, principally composed of a repetition of the first cadence, on pedal point (the time being augmented), lead to the appearance of the 2nd subject.

D. The 2nd subject begins in E♭ minor instead of in E♭ major. It is divided into 3 parts:—1st part, bars 41-79 (beginning in E♭ minor); 2nd part, bars 79-103 (in E♭ major); 3rd part, bars 103-111 (in E♭ major).

E. The Coda contains a portion of the 1st subject in E♭ major, it ends on the 1st inversion of the dominant 7th of G minor, bar 124.

F. The development commences in G minor with the first 2 bars of the introduction, the 2nd of which is repeated, bar 127, and at the end of it there is an enharmonic modulation (E♭-D♯) into E minor. The introduction is again referred to, bars 132-133 and 138-139, the figure used being undoubtedly taken from it. The development, however, has reference principally to the 1st subject.

G. The connecting episode begins with a repetition of the first 4 bars of the 1st subject, and is formed principally upon bars 5-6 of the same subject. Excepting at the commencement and at the close, it quite differs from the original connecting episode.

H. The first part of the 2nd subject (instead of being in C minor) re-appears first in F minor, bars 213-229. At bar 229 it, as well as the other parts, occurs in the tonic key.

J. The Coda commences with a portion of the 1st subject, followed by 4 bars "Grave," derived from the introduction, ending with a final reference to the 1st subject.

SECOND MOVEMENT.

A. Some writers consider this movement in Ternary Form.[*]

B. The 1st subject of 8 bars ending on full close in the tonic is repeated (varied) an 8th higher, bars 9-16.

C. This episode begins, bar 16, in F minor, but at bar 20 it modulates to E♭, the dominant.

D. The 1st subject re-appears without the varied repetition (see note A).

E. This episode commences in A♭ minor. In it are two instances of enharmonic modulation : at bar 42, where it modulates to E major, in which key the first part is repeated, and at bar 48 (the modulation here being from the key of E major into the chord of the dominant minor 9th of E♭). This chord is followed by dominant harmony (chords of the 11th and dominant 7th) leading into the third appearance of the 1st subject in tonic key. At the commencement of this episode the rhythm of the harmony of the accompaniment is changed into triplets, and continues so to the end of the movement.

F. The 1st subject is repeated an 8th higher (as at the commencement), bar 59.

THIRD MOVEMENT.

A. The 1st subject ends bar 9, bars 10-18 being only a continuation of it.

B. This episode is in sequential form, a phrase in F minor, bars 19-22, being repeated (with slight alterations) in E♭ major, bars 23-26.

C. The 2nd subject is considered by some writers to extend to bar 52.[†]

D. After the 2nd subject there is a passage leading back to tonic key ending on dominant 7th, it is constructed mainly upon a part of the 2nd subject (bars 34[(9)]-35[(1)]).

E. The 3rd subject, bars 79-87, is varied, bars 88-95. After 4 bars of imitation it appears again (varied), bars 100-108.

F. After the 2nd variation of the 3rd subject, ending on the dominant, bar 108, there is a passage of 14 bars on dominant pedal point preparatory to the third entry of the 1st subject.

G. The 1st subject re-appears *without* the "continuation" referred to at "A."

H. This episode is built upon the 6th and 7th bars of the 1st subject. It is sequential in form, bars 130-131 in C minor being repeated, bars 132-133. It then modulates, by the aid of the augmented 6th, to the key of C major, in which key the 2nd subject immediately begins.

J. The connecting passage (see D) is altered and prolonged, bars 154-172[(1)].

K. The "continuation" of the 1st subject (see note A) is varied and curtailed.

L. The Coda begins with a passage, bars 183-187, founded upon a part of the 2nd subject (bar 34) varied and lengthened, bars 187-194. It is followed by a passage in C minor, bars 194-203, modulating by means of the Neapolitan 6th (bar 199) to the dominant 7th of A♭ major, the passage ends on pause, bar 203, and a final reference to the 1st subject in the key of A♭ major (repeated); it modulates back to the tonic key by means of the chord of the augmented 6th, bar 208. The movement closes with a descending passage in the harmonic minor scale.

* See "Musical Form," Ebenezer Prout, page 202.
† See Grove's Dictionary, page 156.

(17)

SONATA No. 9.

Op. 14, No. 1.

FIRST MOVEMENT.—"ALLEGRO," KEY OF E MAJOR. SONATA FORM.

ENUNCIATION.	DEVELOPMENT.	RECAPITULATION.
$1 - 13^{(1)}$. 1st subject in E major (tonic). A.	$62 - 92^{(1)}$. E.	$92 - 104$. 1st subject (varied) in original key.
$13 - 22^{(1)}$. Connecting episode. B.		
$22^{(3)} - 57^{1}$. 2nd subject in B major. C.		$104 - 114$. Connecting episode. F.
$57 - 61$. Coda. D.		$114^{(3)} - 149^{(1)}$. 2nd subject in E major (tonic). G.
Double bar and repeat.		
		149. Coda. H.

SECOND MOVEMENT.—"ALLEGRETTO AND MAGGIORE." TERNARY FORM. A.

"Allegretto." Key of E minor. B.	"Maggiore." Key of C major. D.	
1ST PART.	**2ND PART.**	**3RD PART.**
$1-16$. 1st subject in E minor (tonic).	$1-16$. 1st subject in C major, ending in G major.	"Allegretto."
$17-32^{(1)}$. Development.	*Double bar and repeat.*	Da Capo.
$32^{(3)}-51^{(3)}$. 1st subject in original key.	$17-26$. Episode. E.	Coda.
$51-62$. Coda in tonic major key. C.	$27-34$. 1st subject in original key.	
	$35-38$. Connecting passage. F.	

THIRD MOVEMENT.—"ALLEGRO COMMODO," KEY OF E MAJOR. RONDO FORM.

1ST PART.	**2ND PART.**	**3RD PART.**
$1 - 16^{(1)}$. 1st subject in E major (tonic). A.	$49-85^{(1)}$. 3rd subject in G major and E minor. E.	$85^{(3)} - 93^{(3)}$. 1st subject in original key.
$16 - 23^{(1)}$. Episode. B.		$93^{(3)}-100^{(1)}$. Episode. F.
$23^{(3)}-31^{(3)}$. 2nd subject in B major. C.		$100^{(3)}-104^{(1)}$. 2nd subject in A major. G.
$32^{(3)}-40^{(3)}$. 1st subject in original key.		$104^{(3)}-110^{(1)}$. H.
$40^{(3)}-49^{(1)}$. Episode. D.		$110^{(3)}$. 1st subject (varied) in original key. J.

In numbering the bars, each portion of a bar, either at the commencement or in the course of a movement, has been reckoned as one bar; the small figures in brackets denote the beat of the bar to which reference is made.

FIRST MOVEMENT.

A. The 1st subject begins with a sentence of 4 bars upon tonic pedal point. Bar 5 is repeated an 8th lower (bar 6), bar 7 an 8th higher (bar 8), and bars 9-10 an 8th lower (bars 11-12). The end of the 1st subject and the commencement of the connecting episode overlap.

B. The connecting episode commences with the first 2 bars of the 1st subject. It modulates to F♯ major (dominant of 2nd subject) in which key it ends, bar 22.

C. The two 4-bar phrases with which the 2nd subject commences, 22-26 and 26-30 (the 2nd being an imitation of the 1st a note lower), are repeated with slight alterations in the bass, bars 30-38. The 4-bar phrase, 38-42, ending in dominant key is repeated, bars 42-46. A new figure is then introduced, bar 46 which is considered by some writers as the commencement of the Coda. The 2nd subject closes, bar 57, in the dominant key. (Note the consecutive 5ths, bar 53.)

D. The bass of the Coda is formed upon the 1st subject. It modulates at bar 61 from the dominant key back to the tonic.

E. The development begins with a reminiscence of the 1st subject, but after a few bars an important episode is introduced, bars 66-82, in the key of C major. Bars 82-92 are formed on the 1st subject, upon dominant pedal point.

F. The connecting episode is of the same length as the original one, the first 4 bars of which, in the key of C, are varied and the keys altered so as to end in dominant key; it modulates to the dominant, bar 107, by means of the chord of the augmented 6th.

G. The 2nd subject is transposed into the tonic key. (Note the consecutive 5ths, bar 145.)

H. The Coda is based upon the passage in bars 57-61. (See D.)

SECOND MOVEMENT.

A. " Menuetto and Trio," though not so designated.

B. The "Allegretto" (Menuetto) is in Simple Binary form.

C. The Coda consists of a figure, bars 52-53, taken from the 1st subject (bars 12-13), which is repeated 5 times on a tonic pedal point.

D. The 1st part of the " Maggiore " (Trio) is in Simple Binary form.

E. This episode is formed upon a pedal point on G (the dominant).

F. The 2nd movement ends at bar 34, followed by 4 bars (34-38) modulating back to the key of tonic (E minor). Bars 27-38 occur again in the Coda.

THIRD MOVEMENT.

A. The 1st subject begins with section of 4 bars ending on dominant 7th followed by 2 sections (the 2nd being an exact transposition of the former an eighth lower) of 2 bars each, forming a complete sentence in E. The 1st subject ends bar 9. Bars 10-16 consist of a repetition of the 1st subject (shortened).

B. This episode is principally based upon a figure borrowed from the 1st subject, bar 5. It is entirely in the key of the dominant.

C. The 2nd subject, bars 23$^{(3)}$-27$^{(3)}$, is repeated (slightly varied), bars 27-31. It consists of a 4-bar sentence in B major.

D. This episode begins with a reminiscence of 1st subject in E minor, and modulates to G major, on the dominant (pedal point) of which key the figure employed in the 1st episode (letter B) occurs.

E. The 3rd subject is derived from the triplet accompaniment to the 1st subject.

F. This episode resembles the 1st episode transposed into the key of A.

G. Instead of being in tonic key the 2nd subject re-appears in A major.

H. These bars constitute a passage formed upon the 2nd subject leading back to the tonic key.

J. The varied appearance of the 1st subject has all the elements of a Coda. The figure upon which the episodes are formed (already referred to letter B), re-appears at the end of the movement, bars 127-128.

(19)

SONATA No. 10.

Op. 14, No. 2.

FIRST MOVEMENT.—"ALLEGRO," KEY OF G MAJOR. SONATA FORM.

ENUNCIATION.	DEVELOPMENT.	RECAPITULATION.
1 — 9$^{(1)}$. Subject in G major (tonic). A.		126$^{(8)}$—134$^{(1)}$. 1st subject in original key.
9$^{(4)}$—26. Connecting episode. B.	65—126$^{(1)}$. E.	134$^{(1)}$—154. Connecting episode. F.
27 — 48$^{(1)}$. 2nd subject in D major. C.		155 — 176$^{(1)}$. 2nd subject in G major
48 — 64. Coda. D.		(tonic).
Double bar and repeat.		176. Coda. G.

SECOND MOVEMENT.—"ANDANTE," KEY OF C MAJOR. AIR WITH VARIATIONS.

AIR.	1ST VARIATION.	2ND VARIATION.	3RD VARIATION.	CODA.
1—22. A.	23—45. B.	45$^{(6)}$—71$^{(1)}$. C.	71—91$^{(1)}$. D.	91. E.

THIRD MOVEMENT.—"ALLEGRO ASSAI," "SCHERZO," KEY OF G MAJOR. RONDO FORM.

1ST PART.	2ND PART.	3RD PART.
1—23. 1st subject in G major (tonic). A.	74—125$^{(1)}$. 3rd subject in C major. D.	139$^{(8)}$—161$^{(1)}$. 1st subject in original key.
24—42. 2nd subject in E minor, ending in G major. B.	125$^{(8)}$—139$^{(1)}$. E.	161$^{(8)}$—190$^{(1)}$. F.
43—65$^{(1)}$. 1st subject in original key.		190$^{(1)}$—238$^{(1)}$. Episode. G.
65—74$^{(1)}$. C.		238. 1st subject (curtailed) in original key. H.

ALTERNATIVE SCHEME, TERNARY FORM.

1ST PART.	2ND PART.	3RD PART.
1—65. 1st subject in G major.	74—125. 2nd subject in C major.	139—190. Repetition of 1st part (shortened).
65—74. Modulating passages.	125—139. Modulating passages.	190. Coda.

In numbering the bars, each portion of a bar, either at the commencement or in the course of a movement, has been reckoned as one bar; the small figures in brackets denote the beat of the bar to which reference is made.

FIRST MOVEMENT.

A. The 1st subject consists of an 8-bar sentence in tonic key throughout, the first 4 bars being all in the same rhythm.

B. The last 6 bars of the melodious connecting episode are constructed upon a pedal point on A, reached by a gradually rising bass from G to the 9th above, the melody being also in sequence.

C. The 2nd subject in D major is composed of two sections of 4 bars each, the 1st ending on dominant 7th, the 2nd on chord of D major overlapping a new phrase of one bar, which is repeated 3 times, the 3rd repetition being altered to end in A major; the same phrase recurs again leading to a modulation to G major, followed by a passage leading back to D major.

D. The Coda is composed of new material of the nature of a supplementary subject.

E. The development, commencing in G minor, refers to both the 1st and 2nd subjects. It ends on dominant 7th after 14 bars on dominant pedal point.

F. The connecting episode re-appears altered so as to end on the dominant.

G. The Coda resembles that in the enunciation for several bars, after which a variation of the 1st subject occurs on tonic pedal point.

SECOND MOVEMENT.

A. The " Air " is in 2-bar rhythm.

B. In the 1st variation there is syncopation in nearly every bar.

C. The 2nd variation contains several instances of pedal point.

D. The 3rd variation is characterised by a persistent semiquaver figure, the harmony being exactly the same as in the enunciation of the air.

E. The Coda contains slight reminiscences of the original theme.

THIRD MOVEMENT.

A. The 1st subject begins with a sentence of 8 bars in G major followed by a section of 8 bars built entirely upon the chord of the dominant 7th, the 1st sentence then re-appears curtailed to 6 bars.

B. The 2nd subject is in 4-bar rhythm, and is constructed upon bars 24-27, ending in A minor, bar 39, followed by the chord of the dominant 7th.

C. After the second entry of the 1st subject there are 8 bars of the chord of the dominant 7th (bars 65-73) preparatory to the entry of the 3rd subject.

D. The 3rd subject commences with a sentence of 8 bars ending with full close in C major, which is repeated. A passage in 4-bar rhythm, principally on dominant pedal point, (of C major) closing in G, leads to the re-appearance of the first sentence. The last 2 bars are repeated twice, forming a little Codetta.

E. The 14 bars (125-139) formed upon the 1st subject ending on dominant, lead to the third entry of the 1st subject.

F. Twenty-nine bars of a fragmentary character, built upon the 1st subject, occur before the succeeding episode, bars 161-190.

G. This episode takes the place of the repetition of the 2nd subject, it begins and ends in G major (tonic), and is based upon bars 191-192.

H. There is a tonic pedal point from bar 238 to the end.

SONATA No. 11.

OP. 22.

FIRST MOVEMENT.—"ALLEGRO CON BRIO," KEY OF B♭ MAJOR. SONATA FORM.

ENUNCIATION.	DEVELOPMENT.	RECAPITULATION.
1 — 12$^{(2)}$. 1st subject in B♭ major (tonic). A.	70—129$^{(1)}$. E.	129$^{(4)}$—140$^{(3)}$. 1st subject in original key.
12$^{(4)}$—22. Connecting episode. B.		140$^{(4)}$—154. Connecting episode. F.
23 — 57. 2nd subject in F major. C.		155 — 189$^{(1)}$. 2nd subject in B♭ major (tonic).
57—69. Coda. D.		189. Coda. G.
Double bar and repeat.		

SECOND MOVEMENT.—"ADAGIO CON MOLT' ESPRESSIONE," KEY OF E♭ MAJOR. SONATA FORM.

ENUNCIATION.	DEVELOPMENT.	RECAPITULATION.
1 — 12. 1st subject in E♭ major (tonic).	32—48$^{(1)}$. B.	48 — 58$^{(1)}$. 1st subject (varied) in original key. C.
13 — 19$^{(1)}$. Connecting episode. A.		58$^{(4)}$—66$^{(1)}$. Connecting episode. D.
19$^{(2)}$—28. 2nd subject in B♭ major.		66$^{(2)}$—75$^{(1)}$. 2nd subject in E♭ major (tonic).
28 — 31. Coda.		75$^{(1)}$. Coda.

THIRD MOVEMENT.—"MENUETTO AND MINORE." TERNARY FORM.

Menuetto. Key of B♭ major. A. Minore (Trio). Key of G minor. B.

1ST PART.		2ND PART.		3RD PART.
1 — 9. 1st subject commencing in B♭ major (tonic).		1 — 9. 1st subject in G minor, ending in D minor.		Menuetto Da Capo.
Double bar and repeat.		Double bar and repeat.		
10 — 18$^{(1)}$. Episode.		10 -- 14$^{(1)}$. Development.		
18$^{(3)}$—·26$^{(1)}$. 1st subject (varied) in original key.		14$^{(2)}$.—18. 1st subject (shortened) in original key, altered so as to end in G minor.		
26$^{(2)}$- ·32. Coda.		Double bar and repeat from bar 10.		
Double bar and repeat from bar 10.				

FOURTH MOVEMENT.—"ALLEGRETTO," KEY OF B♭ MAJOR. RONDO FORM.

1ST PART.	2ND PART.	3RD PART.
1 — 19$^{(1)}$. 1st subject in B♭ major (tonic). A.	68$^{(2)}$—112. E.	113 — 130$^{(1)}$. 1st subject (varied) in original key.
19$^{(2)}$—23. Episode. B.		130 — 136. Episode. F.
23$^{(2)}$— 41$^{(1)}$. 2nd subject in F major. C.		136 — 153$^{(2)}$. 2nd subject in B♭ major (tonic). G.
41$^{(1)}$—50$^{(2)}$. D.		153 -- 165$^{(2)}$. H.
50$^{(4)}$—68$^{(1)}$. 1st subject in original key.		165$^{(4)}$—183$^{(1)}$. 1st subject (varied) in original key.
		183$^{(2)}$. Coda. J.

In numbering the bars, each portion of a bar, either at the commencement or in the course of a movement, has been reckoned as one bar; the small figures in brackets denote the beat of the bar to which reference is made.

(22)

FIRST MOVEMENT.

A. The 1st phrase of the first subject only consists of $3\frac{1}{2}$ bars, and the rhythm of it seems incomplete. Three silent beats at the beginning would make the phrase 4 bars, and therefore well defined; or the first 3 beats of bar 5 may be considered as belonging to the 1st phrase as well as to the 2nd phrase, the end of the former overlapping the latter. The 1st subject ends on the dominant. The 1st subject may possibly end at bar $9^{(1)}$.

B. The connecting episode begins (with a figure borrowed from bars 3-4) in the tonic key, soon after followed by 2 bars in sequence, leading to 6 bars on pedal point (key of C major).

C. The 1st bar of the 2nd subject is accompanied by the passage which links the connecting episode to it, transposed a fifth lower. This subject is divided into three portions—1st portion, bars $23\text{-}31^{(1)}$; 2nd portion, $31^{(m)}\text{-}44$; 3rd portion, 45-57. The 3rd portion begins very abruptly at bar 45, and robs the 2nd portion of the completion of its last phrase.

D. The beginning of the Coda is taken from the 2nd portion of the 2nd subject, upon pedal point.

E. The development is principally formed upon the Coda and the figure at the commencement of the 1st subject; it closes upon the dominant 7th.

F. The connecting episode is altered so as to end in the dominant key, instead of the key of C, as before.

G. The original Coda is almost literally transposed into tonic key.

SECOND MOVEMENT.

A. The connecting episode is not constructed upon previous material, but is in the form of an episode beginning in tonic key and modulating to the dominant.

B. The 2nd subject is not referred to in the development, it being confined to the 1st subject.

C. The last 2 bars of the 1st subject are omitted.

D. The connecting episode is altered to end in tonic key.

THIRD MOVEMENT.

A. The "Minuetto" is in Simple Binary form.

B. The "Trio" is in Simple Binary form.

FOURTH MOVEMENT.

A. The 1st subject commences with a section of 8 bars, ending in the dominant key, which is repeated (varied), ending in tonic key, bar 17, two more bars being added, ending with full close in tonic key.

B. This modulating episode consists of a new figure in tonic key, modulating to the dominant key.

C. The last 8 bars of the 2nd subject consist entirely of arpeggio chords in the right hand in demisemiquavers, and the same in the left hand in quavers, the first 5 bars of which are built upon tonic pedal point (of F major).

D. Bars 41-50 constitute a passage of imitation formed on figure of 1st subject, leading back to tonic key.

E. The 2nd part begins with the figure of the episode (letter B), which forms an important part in this development, bars 81-95. A new subject is introduced, bars 73-81, repeated in B♭ minor, 96-104. Bars 104-112 form a passage leading back to tonic key.

F. This episode is constructed upon the same material as the original one (letter B), altered so as to end in tonic key, instead of the dominant.

G. The concluding part of the 2nd subject is altered; instead of ending in the key in which it begins, as it originally did, it modulates to the key of E♭, and leads into a transient return of the 1st subject.

H. Bars 153-165 form a passage founded upon 1st subject leading to the final entry of that subject.

J. At the commencement of the Coda a new figure is introduced, it ends with a reference to the 1st subject.

SONATA No. 12.

Op. 26.

FIRST MOVEMENT.—"Andante," key of A♭ major. Air with Variations. A.

Air. B.	1st Variation. C.	2nd Variation. D.	3rd Variation. E.	4th Variation. F.	5th Variation. G.
Key of A♭ major, 1—35.	Key of A♭ major, 1—35.	Key of A♭ major, 1—35.	Key of A♭ minor, 1—35.	Key of A♭ major, 1—35.	Key of A♭ major, 1—35. 36. Coda.

SECOND MOVEMENT.—"Allegro Molto," "Scherzo and Trio." Ternary Form.

Scherzo. Key of A♭ major. A.		Trio. Key of D♭ major.	
1st Part.		**2nd Part.**	**3rd Part.**
1 — 17. 1st subject begins in E♭ major, B, ends in A♭ major (tonic). *Double bar.*		1 — 9. 1st subject in D♭ major, ending in A♭ major. *Double bar and repeat.*	
18 — 46⁽¹⁾. Episode. C.		10—26. Episode. E.	Scherzo. Da Capo.
46⁽¹⁾—62⁽¹⁾. 1st subject (varied) in original keys. D.		*Double bar and repeat from bar 10.* 27—31. F.	
62⁽¹⁾. Coda.			
Double bar and repeat from bar 18.			

THIRD MOVEMENT.—"Maestoso Andante," "Marcia Funèbre sulla Morte d'un Eroe," key of A♭ minor. Ternary Form.

1st Part.	2nd Part. B.	3rd Part.
1—31. Subject in A♭ minor (tonic). A.	32—40⁽¹⁾. Subject in A♭ major.	40⁽¹⁾—70. Repetition of 1st part. 70. Coda. C.

FOURTH MOVEMENT.—"Allegro," key of A♭ major. Rondo Form.

1st Part.	2nd Part.	3rd Part.
1 — 29⁽¹⁾. 1st subject in A♭ major (tonic). A.	81⁽¹⁾—98⁽¹⁾. 3rd subject in C minor, ending in E♭ major. E.	102⁽¹⁾—130. 1st subject in original key.
29⁽¹⁾—33⁽¹⁾. Episode. B.		130⁽¹⁾—140⁽¹⁾. Episode. G.
33⁽¹⁾—49. 2nd subject in E♭ major. C.	98⁽¹⁾—102. F.	140⁽¹⁾—156⁽¹⁾. 2nd subject in A♭ major (tonic).
49 — 53. D.		156⁽¹⁾. Coda. H.
53⁽¹⁾—81. 1st subject in original key.		

In numbering the bars, each portion of a bar, either at the commencement or in the course of a movement, has been reckoned as one bar; the small figures in brackets denote the beat of the bar to which reference is made.

FIRST MOVEMENT.

A. The 1st movement is not in regular Sonata form; the only other exceptions are Op. 27, No. 1 and No. 2 ; Op. 54, and Op. 109. There is no movement in Sonata form in Op. 26.

B. The "Air" is composed of two sections of 8 bars each, 1-9 and 9-17, ending on full close in the tonic ; it is followed by 2 bars in B♭ minor, 17-19 ; treated in sequence, 19-21 ; and 6 bars modulating to the dominant, 21-27, after which the 2nd section of the air is repeated, bars 28-35.

C. 1st variation. Characterised by a demisemiquaver figure which pervades it.

D. 2nd variation. The " Air " (varied) appears in the bass.

E. 3rd variation. Syncopation is employed throughout.

F. 4th variation. Syncopation is freely used. The principal accent occurs on the third beat of each bar.

G. 5th variation. At the close of the variation there is a Coda, bar 36 to the end.

SECOND MOVEMENT.

A. The " Scherzo " is in Simple Binary form.

B. The 1st subject begins in the key of the dominant instead of in the tonic (*see* also " Allegretto," Op. 27, No. 2) ; bars 1-9 are repeated (varied), bars 9-17.

C. The episode begins with a sequence of 8 bars formed upon the 1st subject.

D. The 1st subject re-appears in the bass, with a running quaver accompaniment in the treble ; it afterwards (bar 54) appears in the treble, the quaver accompaniment being in the bass.

E. This sequential episode is formed on the rhythm of the 1st subject.

F. A modulating passage of 4 bars, 27-31, leads back to the resumption of the 1st subject.

THIRD MOVEMENT.

A. The 1st subject commences in A♭ minor, it modulates (bar 8) to C♭ (relative major), at bar 10 to B minor, at bar 16 to D major, and at bar 19 to E♭ major. At bar 22 the 1st part of the subject is repeated altered so as to end in A♭ minor (tonic).

B. The 2nd part is divided into two portions of 4 bars each (both repeated), the former of which ends in the key of E♭ major.

C. Note the double counterpoint, bars 70-73. The part next the bass, bars 70-71, is in the treble, bars 72-73, and the treble of bars 70-71 is in the part next the bass, bars 72-73. The whole of the Coda is upon a pedal point.

FOURTH MOVEMENT.

A. The 1st subject is curiously constructed ; the first portion of it, to bar 13, is in 3-bar rhythm, the last portion, bars 13-29, in 2-bar rhythm (excepting bars 17$^{(m)}$-21$^{(m)}$, which are in 4-bar rhythm) ; it abounds in inversions and imitations.

B. The episode is composed of a sequence formed on the 1st subject ; bars 29$^{(m)}$-31$^{(1)}$ are repeated in the treble, bars 31$^{(m)}$-33$^{(1)}$, a 12th higher.

C. The 2nd subject is accompanied by the 1st subject figure.

D. The beginning of the short passage, bars 49-53, on dominant pedal point furnishes the material for the 3rd subject ; it simply leads from the key of the dominant to the key of the tonic.

E. The 3rd subject commences in C minor, bar 81$^{(m)}$. At bar 89 it modulates to G minor (bars 82-89 are repeated). After modulating to the key of F minor it ends, bar 98, in E♭ major.

F. Bars 98-102 form a passage resembling somewhat that at letter D.

G. This episode is very like that at letter B, extended. Instead of ending in B♭ major, it ends on the dominant of tonic key.

H. The Coda is constructed upon tonic pedal point and formed upon the 1st subject.

SONATA No. 13.

Op. 27, No. 1. "Quasi una Fantasia."

FIRST MOVEMENT.—"Andante and Allegro," key of E♭ major. Ternary Form A.

1st Part. "Andante" ₵.	2nd Part. "Allegro" $\frac{6}{8}$.	3rd Part.
1 — 9. 1st subject in E♭ major (tonic). **B.**	39—66. Episode (D) in C major.	67—82. Repetition of 1st subject, "Andante" (varied).
9⁽¹⁾—22. Episode. **C.**		
23 — 38. 1st subject (varied).		83. Coda.

SECOND MOVEMENT.—"Allegro Molto e Vivace," key of C minor. Ternary Form. A.

1st Part. B.	2nd Part.	3rd Part.
1—16. 1st subject begins in C minor (tonic), ends in G minor.	45⁽⁸⁾—61. Subject begins in A♭ major and ends in E♭ major.	82—137⁽¹⁾. Repetition of Part 1 (varied and extended).
Double bar and repeat.	*Double bar and repeat from bar 46.*	
18—26. Episode. **C.**	62 — 80. Episode. **D.**	
27—45⁽¹⁾. 1st subject (varied) in original key, altered so as to end in C minor (tonic).		137—149. Coda.
Double bar and repeat from bar 20.		

THIRD MOVEMENT.—"Adagio con Espressione," key of A♭ major. Ternary Form. A.

1st Part..	2nd Part.	3rd Part.
1—8⁽²⁾. 1st subject in A♭ major (tonic). **B.**	8⁽³⁾—16. Episode C.	17—24. 1st subject (varied) in original key.
		24—26. **D.**

FOURTH MOVEMENT.—"Allegro Vivace," key of E♭ major. Rondo Form.

1st Part.	2nd Part.	3rd Part.
1 — 25⁽²⁾. 1st subject in E♭ major (tonic). **A.**	107—167. Development. **F.**	167⁽¹⁾—191⁽²⁾. 1st subject in original key. **G.**
25⁽²⁾ — 36⁽²⁾. Episode. **B.**		191⁽²⁾—204⁽²⁾. Episode. **H.**
36⁽²⁾ — 73⁽¹⁾. 2nd subject in B♭ major. **C.**		204⁽²⁾—241⁽²⁾. 2nd subject in E♭ major (tonic).
73⁽²⁾ — 83⁽²⁾. Episode. **D.**		241⁽²⁾—256. Episode. **J.**
83 — 98. 1st subject in original key.		257. Coda. **K.**
99 — 107⁽¹⁾. **E.**		

In numbering the bars, each portion of a bar, either at the commencement or in the course of a movement, has been reckoned as one bar; the small figures in brackets denote the beat of the bar to which reference is made.

(26)

FIRST MOVEMENT.

A. This is the second Sonata of which the first movement is not in Sonata form, the first instance under our notice being Op. 26.

B. The first subject consists of two complete sentences in E♭ major of four bars each—both of which are repeated.

C. This episode, like the first subject, begins and ends in the key of the tonic, it modulates, bars 15-16, to F minor, bars 15-18 are repeated (slightly varied), bars 19-22.

D. This episode commences with an 8-bar section, ending in the key of G major, bar 47 (double bar and repeat from bar 39), followed by another 8-bar section (founded upon the above), with a varied repetition of the same. leading into the key of the tonic E♭.

SECOND MOVEMENT.

A. This movement resembles a " Minuet and Trio," though it is not so designated.

B. This part (Menuetto) is in Simple Binary form.

C. The episode is formed upon the 1st subject.

D. This episode is entirely formed upon the chord of the dominant 9th, the rhythm being the same as in the preceding part.

THIRD MOVEMENT.

A. This movement may be considered an introduction to the 4th movement.

B. The first subject ends on half-close on the dominant.

C. This episode begins and ends in the key of the dominant. In the concluding bar (16) there is a modulation back to the tonic key.

D. Bars 24-26 constitute a cadenza leading into the 4th movement.

FOURTH MOVEMENT.

A. The 1st subject begins with a 4-bar section ending in dominant key, which is repeated (altered), ending in tonic key, forming a complete sentence of 8 bars ; bars 10-17 form another sentence of 8 bars ; bars 18-25 are a repetition of bars 10-17.

B. This episode is formed upon the beginning of the 1st subject.

C. The 2nd subject is in two parts, both begin and end in the key of the dominant, bars $36^{(1)}$-$57^{(1)}$ and 57-$73^{(1)}$.

D. This episode is formed on dominant pedal point, modulating to tonic key.

E. Bars 99-107, constructed on the 1st subject, begin in the key of tonic minor and end in G♭ major ; they are preparatory to the second part (development), which begins in that key.

F. The 2nd part consists of a working out of the first subject (bars 107-140), followed (bars 140-167) by a passage leading to the 3rd entry of 1st subject.

G. The repetition of part of 1st subject already referred to (letter A) re-appears here inverted, bars 184-191.

H. This episode begins like the 1st (letter B), which it imitates exactly for 4 bars, after which it modulates and ends on dominant, bar 204.

J. This episode resembles letter D. It begins in the key of A♭ major, and ends on dominant 7th, bar 256.

K. The Coda reverts to the 3rd movement transposed into E♭ major (Introduction to the 4th movement), after a cadenza it closes " Presto," bar 267 to the end, formed upon the second and third notes of the 1st subject.

A. SONATA No. 14.

Op. 27. No. 2. Quasi una Fantasia ("Moonlight").

FIRST MOVEMENT.—"Adagio Sostenuto," key of C♯ minor. Modified Sonata Form. B.

Enunciation.	Development.	Recapitulation.
1——5$^{(1)}$. C.	23$^{(4)}$—42$^{(1)}$. F.	42$^{(4)}$—46$^{(1)}$. 1st subject in original keys.
5——9. 1st subject begins in C♯ minor (tonic), ends in E major. D.		46$^{(4)}$—51$^{(1)}$. Connecting episode. G.
10 — 15. Connecting episode. E.		51$^{(4)}$—60$^{(1)}$. 2nd subject begins in C♯ (tonic) major, ends in C♯ minor. H.
15$^{(4)}$—23$^{(1)}$. 2nd subject begins in B major, ends in F♯ minor.		60. Coda. J.

SECOND MOVEMENT.—"Allegretto and Trio." Ternary Form. A.

Allegretto. Key of D♭ major. B.   Trio. Key of D♭ major. E.

1ST PART.	2ND PART.	3RD PART.
1——9$^{(1)}$. 1st subject in A♭ and D♭ major (tonic). C.	1 — 9. 1st subject in D♭ major. *Double bar and repeat.*	Allegretto. Da Capo.
9$^{(4)}$—17. *Repeated (varied).* D.	10—18$^{(1)}$. Episode.	
18 — 26$^{(2)}$. Episode.	18. Reminiscence of 1st subject in original key. F.	
26$^{(2)}$. 1st subject (varied and extended) in original keys. *Double bar and repeat from bar 18.*	*Double bar and repeat from bar 10.*	

THIRD MOVEMENT.—"Presto Agitato," key of C♯ minor. Sonata Form. A.

Enunciation.	Development.	Recapitulation.
1 — 14. 1st subject in C♯ minor (tonic). B.	66—102. F.	103—116. 1st subject in original key. G. H.
15 — 21$^{(1)}$. Connecting episode. C.		117—158$^{(1)}$. 2nd subject in C♯ minor (tonic). J.
21$^{(3)}$—63$^{(1)}$. 2nd subject in G♯ minor. D.		158. Coda. K.
63 — 64. E.		
Double bar and repeat from bar 2.		

In numbering the bars, each portion of a bar, either at the commencement or in the course of a movement, has been reckoned as one bar; the small figures in brackets denote the beat of the bar to which reference is made.

FIRST MOVEMENT.

A. This Sonata begins with a slow movement, the usual movement in quick time being omitted.

B. The form of this movement would perhaps be better described as Irregular Binary Form, but it contains the chief characteristics of Sonata form.

C. Bars 1-5 form an introduction to the 1st subject.

D. Both subjects begin and end in different keys.

E. Bars 9-15 form a passage which fulfils the duty of a connecting episode, although in some respects it may be considered as a continuation of the 1st subject. It begins in E minor and ends in B minor.

F. The development is very short. It only contains one slight reference to the 1st subject, and 12 bars upon a dominant pedal point closing in tonic key.

G. The connecting episode differs from that already referred to (letter E). It begins in E major and ends in C♯ minor.

H. The 2nd subject re-appears considerably altered after the first 4 bars.

J. The Coda refers to the 1st subject in the part next the bass, bars 60-65.

SECOND MOVEMENT.

A. The "Allegretto and Trio" constitute a "Menuetto and Trio." It is unusual for both to be in the same key.

B. The "Allegretto" (Menuetto) is in Simple Binary form.

C. The 1st subject (Part I.) begins in the key of the dominant. *See* also "Scherzo," Op. 26.

D. The repetition takes the place of the usual double bar and repeat

E. The "Trio" is in Simple Binary form.

F. There is no regular return to the 1st subject.

THIRD MOVEMENT.

A. It is a curious fact that there is no modulation to the relative major key in this movement.

B. The 1st subject begins with arpeggio passages in 2-bar rhythm, bars 1-6 (condensed to 1-bar rhythm, bars 7-8), followed by a dominant pedal point, bars 9-14, upon which it ends.

C. The connecting episode is built upon the 1st subject. It begins in C♯ minor (tonic), and ends in G♯ minor.

D. The 2nd subject (instead of being in the relative major) is in G♯ minor, it is divided into two parts, both beginning and ending in G♯ minor:—First part, bars 21-43[1]; second part, bars 43-63[1]. The second part may be again sub-divided into two portions—43-57[1] and 57-63[1].

E. Bars 63-64 simply modulate into C♯ minor for the repeat, and into C♯ major for the development.

F. The development begins with a reference to the 1st subject. At bar 72 a portion of the 2nd subject occurs in F♯ minor—the melody of which is transposed to the bass, bar 76. Bars 88-100 are constructed upon dominant pedal point.

G. The 1st subject re-appears unaltered.

H. The connecting episode (letter C) is omitted.

J. The 2nd subject is transposed into tonic key, one bar (39) being omitted. Compare bars 37-40 with bars 133-135.

K. The Coda begins with a reminiscence of the 1st subject, followed by a passage of diminished 7ths, bars 164-167. At bars 168-177 there is a recurrence of part of the 2nd subject, and after some arpeggios (note the chord of the Neapolitan 6th, bars 180-181) the movement ends with a reference to the end of the 2nd subject, upon tonic pedal point (bar 191).

SONATA No. 15.

Op. 28. "Pastorale."

FIRST MOVEMENT.—"Allegro," key of D major. Sonata Form.

ENUNCIATION.	DEVELOPMENT.	RECAPITULATION.
1 — 39. 1st subject in D major (tonic). A.		270 — 312. 1st subject in original key.
40 — 90. Connecting Episode. B.	164—269. F.	313 — 365[1]. Connecting Episode. G.
90[8]—159[8]. 2nd subject in A major. C. D.		365[8]—435[8]. 2nd subject in D major (tonic).
159[8]—163. E.		435[8]—438. H.
Double bar and repeat.		439. Coda. J.

SECOND MOVEMENT.—"Andante," key of D minor. Ternary Form.

1ST PART.	2ND PART.	3RD PART.
1 — 8. 1st subject in D minor (tonic). A.	24[6]—32. 1st subject in D major, ending in A major.	43—87[1]. Repetition of 1st part (varied).
Double bar and repeat.	Double bar and repeat from bar 25.	87. Coda. E.
10 — 18[1]. Episode. B.	34 — 38. Episode.	
18[1]—24. 1st subject in original key. C.	38[1]—41. 1st subject in original key shortened. D.	
Double bar and repeat from bar 10.	Double bar and repeat from bar 34.	

THIRD MOVEMENT.—"Allegro Vivace," "Scherzo and Trio." Ternary Form.

Scherzo. Key of D major. A. Trio. Key of B minor.

1ST PART.	2ND PART.	3RD PART.
1—32. 1st subject in D major (tonic), ending in A major. B.	1 — 8. 1st subject in B minor, ending in D major. E.	Scherzo. Da Capo.
33—48. Development. C.	Double bar and repeat.	
49—70. 1st subject in original key. D.	9—24. Repetition of 1st subject.	
Double bar and repeat from bar 33.		

FOURTH MOVEMENT.—"Allegro ma non Troppo," key of D major. Rondo Form.

1ST PART.	2ND PART.	3RD PART.
1 — 17[1]. 1st subject in D major (tonic). A.	68[8]—102[1]. 3rd subject in G major and D minor. F.	114[6]—130. 1st subject in original key. H.
17[6]—29. Episode. B.	102 — 114. G.	130[6]—145. Episode. J.
29[8]—44[1]. 2nd subject in A major. C.		145[6]—161[1]. 2nd subject in D major (tonic).
44 — 52. D.		161 — 169. K.
52[6]—68. 1st subject in original key. E.		169[6]. Coda. L.

In numbering the bars, each portion of a bar, either at the commencement or in the course of a movement, has been reckoned as one bar; the small figures in brackets denote the beat of the bar to which reference is made.

FIRST MOVEMENT.

A. The first ten bars of the 1st subject are repeated an 8th higher, 11-20. The next 8 bars, 21-28, are treated in the same way (with slight alterations and elongations), bars 29-39. This subject ends with a full close on tonic.

B. The connecting episode is of great importance; it contains three distinct episodes, bars 40-62, 63-77[1], and 77-90[2].

C. The 2nd subject begins simultaneously with the ending of the last phrase of the connecting episode.

D. The 2nd subject is divided into 2 parts, bars 90[2]-135[1], and 135[2]-159; both begin and end in the dominant key. Some writers consider the 2nd subject begins at bar 63 and ends bar 159; others that it ends at bar 135.

E. Bars 159-162 form a passage leading to the development.

F. The development is almost entirely founded upon bars 7-10 of the 1st subject. Double counterpoint at the 8th is continuously used from bar 184 to 208. There is no reference to the 2nd subject, excepting at the end, where a portion of the 2nd part of the 2nd subject appears (varied) in B major, B minor, and D major. The development ends on dominant 7th, bar 269.

G. The connecting episode begins exactly like the original one, bars 313-337. It ends, however, in the key of A (instead of E). The 2nd part, bars 338-352, and the 3rd part, bars 352-365, are an exact copy of the 2nd and 3rd parts of the original connecting episode transposed a 4th higher, so as to end in D instead of A.

H. Bars 435-438 form a passage leading into Coda.

J. The Coda, formed on tonic pedal point, refers to the 1st subject.

SECOND MOVEMENT.

A. The 1st subject begins with section of 4 bars, ending in D minor, followed by another 4-bar section, beginning in F major, and ending in A minor.

B. This episode is formed upon dominant pedal point.

C. The 1st subject is altered so as to end in tonic key.

D. The 1st subject is altered so as to end in D major.

E. The Coda refers to both subjects.

THIRD MOVEMENT.

A. The Scherzo is in Simple Binary Form.

B. The 1st subject in the key of D major, bars 1-8, is repeated slightly altered, bars 9-16, in the key of the dominant; bars 1-16 are then repeated with slight alterations, bars 17-32.

C. This development is in sequence. The first 4 bars, 33-36, are repeated first of all in A major, bars 37-40, then in B minor, bars 41-44; it closes on dominant 7th, bar 48.

D. The 1st subject is slightly altered and elongated; it closes in D major.

E. The 1st subject in the 2nd part is in two sections of 4 bars each, repeated, bars 9-24, with the 2nd section preceding the 1st section, occurring in this form twice.

FOURTH MOVEMENT.

A. The 1st subject is curiously constructed. The first 4 bars are repeated, 5-9; the next 4 bars, 9[1]-13, are treated in the same way (varied), bars 13[2]-17. The whole of the subject is written upon a tonic pedal point.

B. This episode, formed of arpeggios, begins in D major and ends in E major.

C. The 2nd subject consists of 4 bars, 29[2]-33, repeated (varied), bars 33[2]-37, the rest of the subject being made up of a repetition of bars 36[2]-37[2]. The first bar of the subject leads off in the treble, answered at the 8th below by the alto, and then by the bass.

D. Bars 44-52 form a passage leading to 2nd entry of 1st subject.

E. At bars 57-58 a little figure is added in the treble part (where there were rests originally).

F. The 1st part of the 3rd subject, bars 68[2]-79, might be looked upon as a development of the 1st subject; at bar 80, however, the subject assumes an independence of its own.

G. Bars 102-114 form a passage on dominant pedal point leading to 3rd entry of 1st subject.

H. The figure referred to at letter E is slightly elaborated, bars 119-120.

J. This episode resembles the original one, altered so as to end in A, instead of in E major.

K. Bars 161-169 form a passage leading to Coda.

L. The Coda begins with an allusion to the 3rd subject. At bar 194 the time changes to *Più Allegro*, the bass being the same as that which accompanies the 1st subject.

SONATA No. 16.

Op. 31. No. 1.

FIRST MOVEMENT.—"Allegro Vivace," key of G major. Sonata Form.

Enunciation.	Development.	Recapitulation.
1—27. 1st subject in G major (tonic). A.		196 — 211. 1st subject in original key (curtailed). E.
28—67$^{(1)}$. Connecting episode. B.	112$^{(4)}$—195. D.	
67—99. 2nd subject in B major and minor. C.		211$^{(1)}$—221. Connecting episode. F.
		221 — 269. 2nd subject in E major and minor and G major (tonic). G.
99—111. Coda. C.		
Double bar and repeat from bar 4.		269. Coda. H.

SECOND MOVEMENT.—"Adagio Grazioso," key of C major. Rondo Form.

1st Part.	2nd Part.	3rd Part.
1 — 16$^{(6)}$. 1st subject in C major (tonic). A.	36—65$^{(1)}$. Episode beginning in A♭ major. C.	65 — 80$^{(2)}$. 1st subject (varied) in original key. D.
16$^{(8)}$—26. Episode. B.		80$^{(8)}$—90. Episode. E.
27 — 35. 1st subject (varied) in original key.		91 — 98$^{(1)}$. 1st subject (varied) in original key.
		98. Coda. F.

THIRD MOVEMENT.—"Allegretto," key of G major. Rondo Form.

1st Part.	2nd Part.	3rd Part.
1 — 33$^{(2)}$. 1st subject in G major (tonic). A.		133$^{(8)}$—165$^{(3)}$. 1st subject (varied) in original key. G.
33$^{(3)}$—43$^{(1)}$. Episode. B.	83$^{(8)}$—133$^{(3)}$. F.	165$^{(3)}$—179$^{(1)}$. Episode. H.
43 — 53. 2nd subject in D major. C.		179 — 189$^{(1)}$. 2nd subject in G major (tonic).
53 — 67$^{(8)}$. Episode. D.		189 — 207. Episode. J.
67$^{(8)}$—83$^{(8)}$. 1st subject in original key. E.		207$^{(3)}$. Coda. K.

In numbering the bars, each portion of a bar, either at the commencement or in the course of a movement, has been reckoned as one bar; the small figures in brackets denote the beat of the bar to which reference is made.

FIRST MOVEMENT.

A. The 1st subject modulates to D major (bars 11-12), into F major (bars 12-19), then into C major, eventually ending with full close on tonic (bar 27).

B. The connecting episode commences with a repetition of the final cadence of the 1st subject, bars 28-31, followed at bar 31 by a passage, the commencement of which is taken from bar 3, ending on the dominant, bar 46—at this bar there is a reminiscence of the 1st subject modulating to the dominant of B major.

C. The 2nd subject (instead of being in the dominant key) leads off with a passage of 8 bars in B major, which is partly repeated in the bass, bars 75-78, in B minor. Then follows a series of sequences, bars 79-99, passing through several keys. The Coda begins with a 2-bar figure in B minor, 99-100, which is repeated, bars 101-102, in B major, and again, 103-104, in B minor; the same figure still in B minor continues to the end of the Coda, the time being diminished to one bar.

D. The development does not refer to the 2nd subject, but principally refers to the 1st subject and to the connecting episode (letter B).

E. The modulations to the keys of F and C are omitted (*see* letter A) in the re-appearance of the 1st subject.

F. The connecting episode is very much shortened, and it is altered so as to end on the dominant of E major instead of the dominant of B major.

G. The 2nd subject (which should re-appear in the key of the tonic) commences with the first 8 bars in E major (bars 221-228), partly repeated in E minor (bars 229-236), with a modulation to G major, in which key these same bars re-occur (237-244). Bars 237-269 are a repetition of bars 67-99, harmonically changed.

H. The Coda is extended, bar 282.

SECOND MOVEMENT.

A. The 1st subject ends, bar 8, in the tonic key; bars 9-16 are a repetition of it, ending in the dominant. Alternative scheme: 1st subject, 1-8; bars 8-16, connecting passage.

B. The episode commences with a 3-bar phrase, 16-19, modulating to D minor, repeated, bars 19-22, a tone lower, and is followed by a modulation to the key of the dominant. It ends in that key, bar 26. A cadenza leads back to the tonic key.

C. The 2nd part commences with a new episode in the key of A♭ major, ending bar 54, followed by some passages, principally upon dominant pedal point, suggestive of the episode (letter B), ending with full close on tonic, bars 64-65, simultaneously with the re-entry of the 1st subject.

D. Though the 1st subject is considerably varied, the harmony is unchanged.

E. The same remark (letter D) also applies here as regards the episode. It is unusual for an episode to re-appear without some harmonic change.

F. The Coda is of great interest, principally referring to the 1st subject. Some writers consider this movement to be in Ternary Form.

THIRD MOVEMENT.

A. The 1st subject is in two sections, bars 1-9 and 9-17, it ends bar 17; bars 17-33 being a varied repetition of it.

B. This episode is entirely formed on the initial figure of the 1st subject. It begins in E minor and modulates to D and then to A, in which key it ends, bar 43.

C. The 2nd subject consists of nothing but tonic and dominant harmony; the dominant appearing in an inner part throughout.

D. The episode consists of a passage leading back to the tonic key.

E. The 1st subject re-appears without the repetition (letter A).

F. The development leads off with the 1st phrase of the 1st subject in G minor, in the bass, bars 83-87, followed by some canonical imitations, bars 87-99. The whole of it is based on the 1st subject.

G. In the 3rd entry of the 1st subject, the repetition which was omitted on its 2nd entry (letter E) occurs varied.

H. The original corresponding episode (letter B) is lengthened, and ends in D major instead of in A, as before.

J. This episode, which begins as at letter D, transposed to the tonic key, is here extended, and instead of leading to the return of the 1st subject in its original form, it leads to a Coda, bar 207.

K. The Coda begins with a dominant pedal point, bearing contrapuntal references to the 2nd section of the 1st subject. From bar 225 to the end there are several reminiscences of the 1st subject, which take the place of the regular final return of that subject.

SONATA No. 17.

Op. 31, No. 2.

FIRST MOVEMENT.—" Largo and Allegro," key of D minor. Sonata Form.

ENUNCIATION.	DEVELOPMENT.	RECAPITULATION.
1—6. 1st subject in D minor (tonic). A.		147—156. 1st subject in original key. H.
7—41[(1)]. Connecting episode. B.	97—147[(1)]. G.	157—175[(1)]. Connecting episode. J.
41—63. 2nd subject in A minor. C.		175—197. 2nd subject in D minor (tonic). K.
63—90. Coda. D.		
91—92. E.		197. Coda. L.
95—96. F.		

SECOND MOVEMENT.—" Adagio," key of B♭ major. Modified Sonata Form.

ENUNCIATION.	DEVELOPMENT.	RECAPITULATION.
1—17[(1)]. 1st subject in B♭ major (tonic). A.		43—59[(1)]. 1st subject (varied) in original key. D.
17—30[(1)]. Connecting episode. B.	38—43[(1)]. C.	59—72[(1)]. Connecting episode.
30—38[(1)]. 2nd subject in F major.		72—80[(1)]. 2nd subject in B♭ major (tonic). E.
		80. Coda. F.

THIRD MOVEMENT.—" Allegretto," key of D minor. Sonata Form. A.

ENUNCIATION.	DEVELOPMENT.	RECAPITULATION.
1 — 32[(1)]. 1st subject in D minor (tonic). B.		215[(1)]—230[(1)]. 1st subject (curtailed) in original key.
32 — 44[(1)]. Connecting episode. C.	96—215[(1)]. G.	230 — 272[(1)]. Connecting episode. H.
44[(1)]—68. 2nd subject in A minor. D.		272[(1)]—296. 2nd subject in D minor (tonic). J.
58 — 91. Coda. E.		296. Coda. K.
92 — 95. F.		
Double bar and repeat.		

In numbering the bars, each portion of a bar, either at the commencement or in the course of a movement, has been reckoned as one bar; the small figures in brackets denote the beat of the bar to which reference is made.

FIRST MOVEMENT.

A. The 1st subject begins and ends upon dominant harmony; the first 2 bars, "Largo," play an important part in the course of the movement.

B. The connecting episode begins with a continuation of the 1st subject, ending on full close in the tonic key, bars 7-21, after which a regular theme in D minor is introduced, the first four notes of which are based upon the figure represented by bars 1-2; they are repeated in the bass, on notes rising by conjunct degrees from D to E, the dominant of the key of the 2nd subject. (*See* also Connecting episode, Op. 14, No. 2, 1st Movement.) Alternative scheme: Connecting episode, bars 7-55; 2nd subject, bars 55-63.

C. The 2nd subject, which is in the dominant minor key, instead of being in the relative major (F), is in two parts, bars 41-55 and 55-62. The rhythm of the 1st part is suggested in the "Allegro" part of 1st subject.

D. The Coda is developed from 2nd subject.

E. Bars 91-92 form a passage leading to the repetition of the enunciation.

F. Bars 95-96 form a connecting passage between the enunciation and the development.

G. The development begins with a recitative (Largo), bars 97-102, derived from bars 1-2. The greater part of the succeeding Allegro is of the same character as the regular theme in the connecting episode, which is also formed upon bars 1-2.

H. The 1st subject re-appears, bar 147, with the 2 Largo bars (1-2) extended to 6 bars (147-152), followed by the rest of the subject as in the original.

J. The connecting episode begins for 2 bars as in the original one; after this, however, it is of quite a different character. A recitative of 4 bars, 159-162, gives place to a passage of 4 bars in F♯ minor, 163-166 (enharmonic modulation, 162-163), repeated (167-170) in G minor, and imitated, 171-175, ending upon dominant harmony.

K. At bars $193^{(2)}$-$196^{(1)}$ it is thought that the limited compass of the instrument in Beethoven's time prevented a literal transposition of the passage, bars $59^{(2)}$-$62^{(1)}$.

L. The Coda is extended (bar 223). The last 12 bars consist of nothing but harmony of the tonic chord. It should be noted that the key of the relative major is not used once during the whole of the movement.

SECOND MOVEMENT.

A. The 1st subject consists of 2 sections: the first 8 bars, the second 9 bars.

B. The connecting episode commences with a 4-bar phrase in the tonic key, followed by a modulation to C major upon a pedal point with a characteristic figure.

C. Bars 38-43 take the place of the "working out" portion of the movement, they simply form a passage consisting of dominant harmony upon dominant pedal point.

D. The second section of the 1st subject has a very elaborate variation in the bass, bars 50-59.

E. The connecting episode, 59-72, is transposed so as to end in dominant key.

F. The Coda is formed from previous material, the passage, bars 80-89, being taken from bars 38-43, and the following passage, 89-98, from the 1st subject. The last 6 bars are upon a tonic pedal point; the subdominant, followed by tonic harmony, forming a plagal cadence which often occurs in Codas in conjunction with tonic pedal.

THIRD MOVEMENT.

A. Note that all the movements in this Sonata are written in Sonata Form.

B. The 1st subject is founded upon the initial figure of 4 notes; in fact, the whole movement is constructed upon it and the figure of 2 notes which commences the 2nd subject.

C. The connecting episode begins in D minor, the initial figure appearing in the bass; at bar 36 it modulates to C major, in which key it continues to bar 43, where by means of augmented 6th on F, it modulates to the chord of E major, dominant of A.

D. The 2nd subject, instead of being in the key of the relative major, is in the key of the dominant minor (see letter C, 1st Movement); it begins with a figure of 2 notes, bar $44^{(2)}$ (see letter B).

E. The Coda is a development of the latter part of the 2nd subject.

F. Bars 92-95 form a passage leading to the repetition of the enunciation, and upon its reiteration into the development.

G. The development is characterised by the persistent reiteration of the initial figure rhythm.

H. The connecting episode commences with part of what was originally the concluding section of the 1st subject, bars 16-19, it then modulates to B♭ major; at bars $243^{(2)}$-246 the initial figure appears in the bass in the key of B♭ minor. From bar 244 it resembles the original episode prolonged with harmonic changes. It ends upon the dominant chord.

J. The 2nd subject is literally transposed into the tonic key, excepting that in some bars the melody is slightly altered.

K. The Coda is extended, bar 322; at bar 336 there is a dominant pedal point in the bass, which continues to bar 351, where it appears also in the treble. The 1st subject re-appears, bars $351^{(2)}$-382. After a chromatic scale passage the movement ends with a reiteration of the perfect cadence founded upon the initial figure rhythm.

SONATA No. 18.

OP. 31, No. 3.

FIRST MOVEMENT.—"ALLEGRO," KEY OF E♭ MAJOR. SONATA FORM.

ENUNCIATION.	DEVELOPMENT.	RECAPITULATION.
1 — 29[1]. 1st subject in E♭ major (tonic). A.	89—137[1]. F.	137 — 165[1]. 1st subject in original key. G.
29 — 45[2]. Connecting episode. B.		165 — 169[2]. Connecting episode. H.
45[3]—64. 2nd subject in B♭ major. C.		169[3]—190[1]. 2nd subject in E♭ major (tonic). J.
64 — 86[1]. Coda. D.		190. Coda. K.
86 — 88. E.		
Double bar and repeat.		

SECOND MOVEMENT.—"ALLEGRETTO VIVACE," "SCHERZO, (A), KEY OF A♭ MAJOR. SONATA FORM.

ENUNCIATION.	DEVELOPMENT.	RECAPITULATION.
1—9[3]. 1st subject in A♭ major (tonic). B.	66—108[1]. H.	108 — 116[2]. 1st subject in original key. J.
9[4]—15[1]. Connecting episode. C.		116[4]—122[1]. Connecting episode. J.
15[4]—34[1]. D.		122[4]—141[1]. K.
34[4]—50[1]. 2nd subject, beginning in F major. E.		141[4]—157[1]. 2nd subject, beginning in G♭ major. L.
50 — 56. Coda. F.		157. Coda. M.
56 — 61. G.		
Double bar and repeat.		

THIRD MOVEMENT.—"MODERATO E GRAZIOSO," "MENUETTO AND TRIO." TERNARY FORM A.

Menuetto. Key of E♭ major. Trio. Key of E♭ major. D.

1ST PART.		2ND PART.	3RD PART.
1— 9. 1st subject in E♭ major (tonic). B.	1—9. 1st subject in E♭ major, ending in B♭ major.		Repetition of "Menuetto" (Part 1).
Double bar and repeat from bar 3.	*Double bar and repeat.*		
12—20. 2nd subject in E♭ major (tonic). C.	10 — 16[2]. Development.		
Double bar and repeat from bar 13.	16[2]—24. 1st subject in original key, altered so as to end in E♭ major.		45. Coda. E.
	Double bar and repeat from bar 10.		

FOURTH MOVEMENT.—"PRESTO CON FUOCO," KEY OF E FLAT MAJOR. SONATA FORM.

ENUNCIATION.	DEVELOPMENT.	RECAPITULATION.
1 — 29[1]. 1st subject in E♭ major (tonic). A.	83—174[2]. E.	174[4]—202[1]. 1st subject in original key. F.
29[1]—65[1]. Connecting episode. B.		202[4]—242[1]. Connecting episode. G.
65 — 77[4]. 2nd subject in B♭ major. C.		242 — 266[1]. 2nd subject in G♭ major. H.
77[3]—80. D.		266. Coda. J.
Double bar and repeat.		

In numbering the bars, each portion of a bar, either at the commencement or in the course of a movement, has been reckoned as one bar; the small figures in brackets denote the beat of the bar to which reference is made.

FIRST MOVEMENT.

A. The 1st subject begins upon the 3rd inversion of the chord of the 11th. Bars 1-8 are repeated in a different register at bars 10-17. Bars 18-21 are also repeated (varied), bars 22-25. The first subject ends with a short passage of the nature of a Codetta, bars 25-29[n].

B. The connecting episode commences without any break, and flows right on from the 1st subject, which subject is referred to, bar 33, the 3rd inversion of the chord of the 11th here having a minor 9th instead of a major as before. The connecting episode ends upon F, the dominant of the 2nd subject key.

C. The 2nd subject consists of 8 bars, 45[m]-53, which, after a connecting passage of 4 bars are repeated (varied), bars 57-64.

D. The Coda is constructed of new material, and begins and ends in dominant key; bars 72-76 are simple arpeggios of the triad of B♭, followed, bars 78-81, by arpeggios of the dominant chord of B♭ accompanied by a shake upon the 5th of the chord. Bar 82 is evidently taken from bar 9, and bar 85 from bar 7.

E. Bars 86-88 form a connecting passage formed from the last phrase of the Coda (bars 82-84.)

F. The development begins like the 1st subject upon which it is chiefly founded, it ends with the harmony of F minor.

G. The 1st subject re-appears with the harmony of F minor in the first two bars, 137-138, instead of the 3rd inversion of the 11th (root B♭), as before.

H. The connecting episode re-appears without the reference to the 1st subject, it ends, however, on the dominant (B♭) instead of on F.

J. The connecting passage (bars 53-56) is varied and extended, 177-183.

K. The Coda, which begins like that in the enunciation, transposed into the tonic key, is extended, the additional bars being founded upon the 1st subject.

SECOND MOVEMENT.

A. The Scherzo, which Beethoven sometimes used instead of the Menuetto, does not here take that position, as it is followed by a Menuetto and Trio. This is the only instance in which Beethoven has used 2-4 time for Scherzo.

B. The 1st subject consists of a sentence of 8 bars ending with full close in the tonic, extended to 9 bars by the repetition of the final cadence.

C. The connecting episode simply consists of a passage modulating to F minor, upon the dominant of which it ends, bar 15.

D. The entrance of the 2nd subject is delayed, there is a passage of 4 bars, 15[d]-19, beginning in D♭ and proceeding down to B♭, G♮, and E♭, forming the chord of the dominant 7th, after which the 1st subject and the connecting episode are repeated, bars 20-34.

E. The 2nd subject commences in F major, instead of in the key of the dominant E♭; it will be seen, however, that it ends in that key, bar 50.

F. The Coda might at first sight be looked upon as the 2nd subject, considering that it begins and ends in the key of the dominant, and that the second subject (see letter E) is of indefinite tonality. It is, however, clearly a Coda formed of tonic and dominant harmony. It should be noted that Beethoven's Scherzos are often somewhat irregular as to form.

G. Bars 56-61 form a passage leading to the repetition of the enunciation, after which, with bars 64-65, it leads to the development.

H. The development commences with a part of the 1st subject in the key of F major. After a reference to 2nd subject a portion of the 1st subject appears in the key of C major, bar 85. A new figure is introduced, bars 92-97. After some scale passages it ends in the tonic key, bar 108.

J. The 1st subject and connecting episode re-appear in the original keys.

K. The 1st subject and connecting episode are repeated as before (see letter D), excepting that the 1st subject is varied.

L. The 2nd subject re-appears, beginning in the key of G♭, which is very irregular, ending, however, in the tonic key, bar 157.

M. The Coda is elongated.

THIRD MOVEMENT.

A. The Menuetto and Trio are in the same key, which is unusual. (See also Allegretto and Trio, Op. 27, No. 2.)

B. The 1st subject ends on half-close upon the dominant.

C. The 2nd subject is developed from the 1st subject and is in the same key.

D. The Trio is in Simple Binary form.

E. In the Coda there is another instance (see letter F, Sonata No. 17, 2nd Movement) of the sub-dominant harmony playing an important part in the Coda, making a prolonged plagal cadence.

FOURTH MOVEMENT.

A. The first sentence of the 1st subject ending with full close in the tonic, bar 7, is repeated, 7-13. The 1st subject may be divided into two parts totally different in character :— the first part, bars 1-7 (which is repeated, bars 7-13), and the 2nd part, bars 13-29, both beginning and ending in tonic key.

B. The connecting episode commences with the passage, bars 21-25, transposed into tonic minor key, succeeded by some new material in the key of the dominant, in which key it ends, bar 65.*

C. The 2nd subject is constructed almost entirely upon the common chord of B♭. The rhythm of it is borrowed from the 2nd part of the 1st subject.

D. Bars 77-80 form a passage, consisting of an extension of the chord of the dominant 7th, leading to the repetition of the enunciation, and after that to the development.

E. The development commences with the passage (slightly altered) which precedes it, transposed into the key of G♭. The 2nd part of the 1st subject then appears in that key ; at bar 99 a new figure is introduced in B minor (enharmonic modulation, bars 94-95, G♭—F♯), repeated, bars 107-110, in C minor ; at bars 111-114 in A♭ major ; at bars 115-118 in D♭ major ; the tonic chord of which is treated as a Neapolitan 6th of the key of C, and the figure finally appears in that key, bars 119-122. The 2nd part of the 1st subject is then again reverted to in the key of C. After some further modulations the development ends upon dominant harmony.

F. The first subject re-appears in its original form.

G. The connecting episode commences as before, and is composed of nearly the same matter, transposed for the most part into G♭ major.

H. The 2nd subject re-appears in the key of G♭ major, bar 242, and in the tonic minor key, bar 254, modulating, bar 265, to the key of the dominant.

J. The Coda commences with a prolonged variation upon the chord of the dominant 7th. From bars 284 to the end there are repeated references to the 1st subject.

SONATA No. 19.

Op. 49. No. 1.

FIRST MOVEMENT.—"ANDANTE," KEY OF G MINOR. SONATA FORM.

ENUNCIATION.	DEVELOPMENT.	RECAPITULATION.
1 — 9⁽³⁾. 1st subject in G minor (tonic). A.	35—66⁽¹⁾. E.	66 — 73⁽³⁾. 1st subject in original key.
9⁽⁴⁾—16. Connecting episode. B.		73⁽⁴⁾—81. Connecting episode. F.
17 — 30⁽³⁾. 2nd subject in B♭ major. C.		82 — 99⁽⁴⁾. 2nd subject in G minor (tonic).
30 — 34. Coda. D.		G.
Double bar and repeat.		99. Coda. H.

SECOND MOVEMENT.—"ALLEGRO," KEY OF G MAJOR. RONDO FORM.

1ST PART.	2ND PART.	3RD PART.
1 — 17⁽¹⁾. 1st subject in G major (tonic). A.	97⁽³⁾—104⁽¹⁾. H.	104⁽¹⁾—136⁽¹⁾. 2nd subject in G major (tonic). J.
17⁽³⁾—31⁽¹⁾. Episode, beginning in G minor. B.		136⁽³⁾—154⁽¹⁾. 1st subject in original key. K.
31 — 33⁽¹⁾. C.		154⁽³⁾. Coda. L.
33⁽³⁾—65⁽¹⁾. 2nd subject in B♭ major. D.		
65⁽³⁾—79⁽³⁾. Episode. E.		
79⁽³⁾—81⁽³⁾. F.		
81⁽¹⁾—97⁽¹⁾. 1st subject in original key. G.		

In numbering the bars, each portion of a bar, either at the commencement or in the course of a movement, has been reckoned as one bar ; the small figures in brackets denote the beat of the bar to which reference is made.

* Alternative scheme : Connecting episode, bars 29-35 ; 2nd subject, 35-77.

FIRST MOVEMENT.

A. The 1st subject consists of a section of 8 bars, ending with half-close upon the dominant.

B. The connecting episode begins with the first 4 bars of the 1st subject, after which it modulates into the key of F major, dominant of the relative major.

C. The 2nd subject begins with 2-bar phrase, 17-18, repeated, 8th higher, 19-20, and again at bars 21-22. At bar 22 this phrase overlaps the commencement of a 4-bar phrase, 22-25, repeated (varied and extended), bars 26-30.

D. The Coda is taken from the beginning of 2nd subject.

E. Nearly all of the development is constructed upon fragments of the 2nd subject. Bars 35-50 are in the key of E♭ major, followed by a (transient) modulation to C minor, and then to tonic key, in which it continues to the end, where it closes upon dominant 7th, the C♮ rising to C♯, and then to D. *See* Sonata No. 10, 1st Movement, bar 126.

F. The connecting episode resembles the original one, altered so as to end in dominant key instead of in the key of F.

G. The latter part of the 2nd subject is varied and extended on its re-appearance.

H. The Coda is formed of the same material as that in the enunciation ; but it is extended, the last 8 bars being upon pedal point. The movement ends with a major triad upon the tonic.

SECOND MOVEMENT.

A. The 1st subject consists of an 8-bar sentence, bars 1-9[1], followed by a 4-bar section, bars 9[m]-13[n], after which the 2nd section of the 1st sentence, bars 5[m]-9[n], is repeated, 13[m]-17[n]. It ends with a full close in the tonic key, bar 17.

B. The episode, after 4 bars of introduction, 17-20, begins in G minor, with a 4-bar phrase ending in D minor, bars 21-24. The same phrase is then repeated, varied and extended, modulating to the key of B♭ major, in which it ends, bars 25-31.

C. Bars 31-33[a] form a connecting passage

D. The 2nd subject, instead of being in D major, is in B♭ major. The last part of the 2nd subject bars 49-57, is repeated, bars 57-65.

E. This episode consists of a complete repetition of the previous episode, the last 4 bars, 76-79, being altered to end in G minor instead of in the key of B♭ major.

F. Bars 79-81 form a connecting passage.

G. The 1st subject re-appears in its entirety.

H. The development is of short duration ; it is founded upon the 1st subject and is of a sequential nature, modulating into E minor, C major, A minor, and G major, and ending in the dominant key.

J. The 3rd part, instead of beginning with the 3rd entry of the 1st subject, commences with the repetition of the 2nd subject transposed into the tonic key.

K. The 1st subject is much varied and extended.

L. The Coda is constructed upon tonic pedal point.

SONATA No. 20.

Op. 49, No. 2.

FIRST MOVEMENT.—"Allegro ma non Troppo," key of G major. Sonata Form.

Enunciation.	Development.	Recapitulation.
1 — 12$^{(1)}$. 1st subject in G major (tonic). A.		67$^{(1)}$— 70. 1st subject in original key. F.
12 — 20$^{(1)}$. Connecting episode. B.	53—67$^{(1)}$. E.	71 — 87$^{(1)}$. Connecting episode. G.
20$^{(8)}$—49$^{(1)}$. 2nd subject in D major. C.		87$^{(3)}$—116$^{(1)}$. 2nd subject in G major (tonic). H.
49 — 52. Coda. D.		116. Coda. H.
Double bar and repeat.		

SECOND MOVEMENT.—"Tempi di Menuetto," key of G major. Rondo Form.

1st Part.	2nd Part.	3rd Part.
1 — 21$^{(1)}$. 1st subject in G major (tonic). A.		88$^{(3)}$—108$^{(1)}$. 1st subject in original key. F.
21 — 43$^{(1)}$. Episode B.	68$^{(1)}$—88$^{(1)}$. E.	108$^{(1)}$. Coda. G.
43 — 48$^{(2)}$. C.		
48$^{(1)}$—68$^{(1)}$. 1st subject in original key. D.		

In numbering the bars, each portion of a bar, either at the commencement or in the course of a movement, has been reckoned as one bar; the small figures in brackets denote the beat of the bar to which reference is made.

FIRST MOVEMENT.

A. The 1st subject consists of 2 sections of 4 bars each, bars 1-4 and 8[(m)]-12 (the bars 5-8 being a repetition of the 1st section an 8th higher).

B. The connecting episode, which commences with a reference to the 2nd section of the 1st subject, is in the key of the tonic, except a transient modulation to the dominant at bar 15, at which bar there is a dominant pedal point, which continues to bar 20.

C. The 2nd subject is in two parts. The 1st part, which ends in the key of A major, bars 20-28, is repeated, bars 28-36, altered at the end so as to close in D major. The 2nd part begins and ends in the dominant key, bars 36-49.

D. The Coda is formed upon the connecting episode figure.

E. The development begins in A minor, modulates to E minor, bar 57, and ends in G major, bars 66-67.

F. The 2nd section of the 1st subject (bars 8-12) is omitted, and there is only a partial recurrence of the repetition of the 1st section (*see* letter A).

G. The connecting episode is considerably altered. It commences with the 1st section of the 1st subject (bar 71), but it modulates to C major, bars 74-75, and is extended into a 5-bar phrase. The succeeding part of the episode (bars 75-81) is derived from the 2nd part of the 2nd subject (bars 36-49). It ends with the closing part of the original connecting episode.

H. The 2nd subject and Coda are transposed into the tonic key.

SECOND MOVEMENT.

A. This theme is also used by Beethoven in his Septet.

B. New material is used for this episode; it commences with a 4-bar phrase in the tonic key, followed by a 4-bar phrase in the dominant key ending in A major, bar 29. The bass of bars 22-23 is used in the treble, bars 26-27. At bar 29 a new figure is introduced, also a pedal point upon the dominant of D. The episode ends in the key of D, bar 43.

C. Bars 43-48 form a connecting passage modulating to tonic key.

D. The 1st subject re-appears unaltered.

E. This episode in C major consists of two sections: 1st section, bars 68-72; 2nd section, bars 72-76; both are repeated, but at the close of the 2nd section there is a modulation to G, and it is extended, forming a connecting passage to the 3rd entry of the 1st subject.

F. The re-appearance of the episode (B) and the 4th entry of the 1st subject are omitted.

G. The Coda, which refers to the 1st subject, begins with transient modulations to the keys of C major and A minor, after which it continues in tonic key.

SONATA No. 21.

Op. 53. "Waldstein."

FIRST MOVEMENT.—"Allegro con Brio," key of C major. Sonata Form.

Enunciation.	Development.	Recapitulation.
1 — 13. 1st subject in C major (tonic). A.		158—176$^{(1)}$. 1st subject in original key. G.
14 — 35$^{(1)}$. Connecting episode. B.		176—198$^{(1)}$. Connecting episode. H.
35 — 74. 2nd subject in E major. C.	92—157. F.	198—237. 2nd subject in A major and C major. J.
74 — 82. Coda. D.		237. Coda. K.
82$^{(2)}$—85. E.		
88 — 91. E.		
Double bar and repeat.		

"Adagio molto," key of F major. Introduction to the Second Movement.

1—9. A.	9$^{(4)}$—17$^{(1)}$. B.	17—28. C.

SECOND MOVEMENT.—"Allegretto Moderato," key of C major. Rondo Form.

1st Part.	2nd Part.	3rd Part.
1 — 62$^{(9)}$. 1st subject in C major (tonic). A.	175$^{(3)}$—220. Episode in C minor. F.	313 — 344. 1st subject (shortened) in original key. H.
62$^{(3)}$—70$^{(1)}$. B.	221—312. Development. G.	344$^{(4)}$—378$^{(1)}$. Episode. J.
70$^{(3)}$—98$^{(1)}$. Episode. C.		378 — 402. K.
98$^{(1)}$—113. D.		403. Coda "Prestissimo." L.
114—175$^{(1)}$. 1st subject in original key. E.		

In numbering the bars, each portion of a bar, either at the commencement or in the course of a movement, has been reckoned as one bar; the small figures in brackets denote the beat of the bar to which reference is made.

FIRST MOVEMENT.

A. The 1st subject begins in the tonic key with a section of 4 bars, ending in G major, which is repeated a tone lower (bars 5-8), with the exception of the note A? in bar 8, which is a tone and a-half lower. This is followed by a 4-bar section in C minor and a pause on the dominant. In the space of 13 bars the 1st subject modulates the G major, F major, F minor, and C minor; it ends on half-close upon the dominant, bar 13.

B. The connecting episode begins (bars 14-17) with the 1st section of the 1st subject, which is repeated (bars 18-21) in D and A minor; bar 22 is a repetition of bar 21 with the 6th of the chord raised a semitone, forming an augmented 6th in the key of E minor, upon the dominant (pedal point) of which there follows a brilliant passage in E minor, leading into E major.

C. The 2nd subject may be divided into two parts. The 1st part (bars 35-42) is repeated (varied), bars 43-50. Bars 50-74 constitute the 2nd part. Both parts are in E major (instead of being in the dominant key).

D. The Coda consists of 4 bars, beginning in A minor and ending in E minor; bars 74-77 repeated an octave lower, bars 78-82$^{(1)}$.

(42)

E. Bars 82-85 form a passage leading to the repetition of the enunciation, after which, with the addition of bars 88-91, it leads to the development; it is taken from the concluding part of the 2nd subject.

F. The development, which is very modulatory in character, commences with a reference to the 1st subject, bars 3-4 of which furnish the materials for bars 94-97; also for bars 98-112. In bars 98-100, bars 3 and 4 are compressed into one bar; also in bars 102-104. In bars 101 and 105 only the 4th bar (compressed) is used, bars 106-112 having only the 3rd bar (compressed); bar 113 leads to an elaborate development of the first portion of the second part of the 2nd subject, bars 114-144. A double pedal point on the tonic and dominant (bars 144-157) prepares for the second entry of the 1st subject. This pedal point resembles that to be found at the close of the development of the 1st Movement of Beethoven's Fourth Symphony in B♭.

G. The 1st subject re-appears unaltered until bar 170, at which bar A♭ is used instead of G, and five bars are added, ending, bar 176, in the tonic key.

H. The connecting episode begins as before (compare bars 14-21 with bars 176-183). Bar 22, however, is altered (bar 184), and a bar added—185—leading to the dominant of A minor; bars 186-197 are an exact transposition of bars 23-34.

J. The 2nd subject re-appears in the key of A major. At bars 202-205 it modulates through A minor to C major, in which key it ends (bar 237).

K. The elongation of the Coda (bar 251) is principally formed upon the 1st subject, with one reference to the 2nd subject (bars 286-296).

INTRODUCTION TO SECOND MOVEMENT.

A. Bars 1-9 form an introductory passage (bar 7 is interpolated into the rhythm); it is sequential in form and modulatory; it begins and ends in the tonic key.

B. At bar 9$^{(a)}$ a melody commences of 8 bars—9$^{(a)}$-17$^{(b)}$.

C. At bar 17 (overlapping the end of the melody), there is a recurrence of the opening passage, which is developed, and which forms another passage ending on the dominant of C, preparatory to the entry of the 1st subject of the Rondo.

SECOND MOVEMENT.

A. Nearly the whole of the 1st subject (which begins and ends in the tonic key) is based upon the initial phrases, which are repeated with a varied accompaniment at bar 31 and at bar 55. Note the shake formed on inverted pedal point, bars 51-62.

B. Bars 62-70 form a connecting passage.

C. At the concluding part of this episode in A minor there is a pedal point in the bass, bars 87-98.

D. Bars 98-113 form a passage leading back to the tonic key, formed on 1st subject.

E. The 1st subject re-appears here unaltered.

F. This episode begins with a subject of 8 bars (175$^{(a)}$-183$^{(a)}$), which proceeds in sequence for 4 bars. The first phrase of 8 notes in C minor is repeated in F minor (177$^{(a)}$-179$^{(b)}$). The first 4 notes are then used to commence a modulation to A♭ major, the subject ending in that key (183$^{(a)}$). Bars 175$^{(a)}$-183$^{(a)}$ are then repeated with a triplet accompaniment (183$^{(m)}$-191$^{(b)}$). This subject is then inverted as regards its harmonic character; instead of the keys being in this order—C minor, F minor, and A♭ major—the subject appears, bars 191$^{(m)}$-199$^{(a)}$, in A♭ major, modulating to F minor and ending in C minor. Bars 191$^{(m)}$-199$^{(a)}$ are repeated (inverted), bars 199$^{(m)}$-207$^{(m)}$, the triplet accompaniment in the upper part being (with slight alterations) transferred to the underpart; bars 203$^{(m)}$-207$^{(a)}$ are repeated (inverted), bars 207$^{(a)}$-211$^{(b)}$; a reiteration of the final cadence brings the episode to a close in C minor.

G. The development begins in A♭ major with reference to the 1st subject (in chords), 221-224, repeated in F minor, 225-228, and in D♭ major, 229-232. A sequence in syncopation leads to a new figure (bar 251); this modulates through several keys, and gives place (bar 269) to another figure, which eventually modulates to C minor (bar 277). Bars 295-312 consist entirely of dominant harmony, and end with full close in the tonic key (bar 313).

H. The first subject is shortened, the first 31 bars being omitted.

J. This episode is formed upon the connecting passage, bars 62-70. Bars 344-352 are varied and extended, bars 352$^{(a)}$-377.

K. A connecting passage (bars 378-402) upon dominant pedal point leads to the Coda, " Prestissimo."

L. The Coda is based almost entirely upon the 1st subject. It is referred to (in the original key), bars 403-406; varied, bars 407-410. In the key of F, bars 427$^{(a)}$-428; varied, bars 429$^{(a)}$-430. In original key, bars 431-434; varied, bars 441-464. In the keys of C major (tonic), C minor, A♭ major, and F minor, bars 485-506; and in original key, bars 515-522. There are sequences in bars 411-427 and bars 434-440.

SONATA No. 22.

Op. 54.

FIRST MOVEMENT.—"Tempi d'un Menuetto," key of F major. Rondo Form. A.

1st Part.	2nd Part.	3rd Part.
1 — 25$^{(1)}$. 1st subject in F major (tonic). B.		106$^{(8)}$—137. 1st subject (varied) in original key. G.
25$^{(3)}$—63$^{(1)}$. Episode. C.	94$^{(8)}$—106$^{(1)}$. Episode. F.	137$^{(1)}$. Coda. H.
63 — 71. D.		
70$^{(8)}$—94$^{(1)}$. 1st subject in original key. E.		

SECOND MOVEMENT.—"Allegretto," key of F major. Modified Sonata Form. A.

Enunciation.	Development.	Recapitulation.
1—13$^{(1)}$. 1st subject in F major (tonic). B.		116—165$^{(1)}$. 1st subject in F major (tonic). F.
13—19. Accessory bars in C major. C.	22—115. E.	
20—21. D.		165. Coda. G.

Alternative Scheme.

1st Part.	2nd Part.	3rd Part.
1 — 9. 1st subject in F major.		116—124. 1st subject in F major, altered to end in B flat.
9—12. Connecting episode.	22—115. Development.	124—135. Connecting episode.
13—17. 2nd subject in C major.		135—138. 2nd subject altered to F major.
17—19. Coda.		139—163. Connecting episode.
20—21. Modulating bars.		165. Coda.

In numbering the bars, each portion of a bar, either at the commencement or in the course of a movement, has been reckoned as one bar; the small figures in brackets denote the beat of the bar to which reference is made.

FIRST MOVEMENT.

A. Rondo form is unusual for the 1st movement of a Sonata.

B. The 1st subject contains a considerable amount of imitation. The sentence, bars 1-5[i], is repeated at bars 5[i]-9[i], and bars 9[i]-17 at 17[i]-25[i]. It ends with full close in the tonic, bar 25[i].

C. This episode is canonical in character; the whole of it is based upon the new subject, which commences in tonic key, bar 25[i], and is imitated in the treble, bar 26[i], at the 8th. It ends upon the dominant, bar 63[i].

D. Bars 63-71[i] form a passage leading to and overlapping the 2nd entry of the 1st subject.

E. The 1st subject is varied on its re-appearance, bar 70[i].

F. This episode resembles that in the 1st part, but it is considerably shortened.

G. The 1st subject is again varied and also extended, ending with a cadenza, bar 137.

H. The Coda refers to the 1st subject and is constructed on pedal point.

SECOND MOVEMENT.

A. This movement consists of a series of repetitions of the subject announced in the bass, bars 1-4, and the sequence, bars 9-12, interspersed with short episodes. It closely conforms to the Toccata form,[*] inasmuch as one subject is repeated over and over again in contrapuntal style; but it more nearly resembles Sonata Form than any other, although only the barest outline is followed.

B. The 1st subject commences with a passage of 4 bars in the bass, repeated in the treble 2 bars behind. The bass of bars 5-6 is repeated in the treble of bars 7-8. A sequence follows, ending in C major.

C. The accessory bars take the place of the 2nd subject; they are founded upon bar 1, beginning with pedal point in the bass.

D. Bar 20 leads to the repetition of the enunciation, bar 21 to the development.

E. The development consists of nothing but repetitions of the 1st subject in various keys, connected by episodes formed (principally) upon the 1st subject.

F. The 1st subject is in the original key upon tonic pedal point; it is considerably altered and extended.

G. The Coda simply refers to the 1st subject. Bars 165-173[i] are repeated with 2 bars added, 173-183[i].

[*] *See* " Musical Forms." (Pauer).

SONATA No. 23.

Op. 57. "Appassionata."

FIRST MOVEMENT.—"Allegro Assai," key of F minor. Sonata Form.

Enunciation.	Development.	Recapitulation.
1.— 17$^{(1)}$. 1st subject in F minor (tonic). A.		136$^{(4)}$—152$^{(1)}$. 1st subject in original key. E.
17$^{(4)}$—36$^{(1)}$. Connecting episode. B.	66$^{(4)}$—136. D.	152 — 175. Connecting episode. F.
36$^{(4)}$—62. 2nd subject beginning in A♭ major. C.		175 — 201. 2nd subject beginning in F major (tonic). G.
62 — 66. Coda.		201. Coda. H.

SECOND MOVEMENT.—"Andante con Moto," key of D♭ major. Air with Variations.

Air.	1st Variation.	2nd Variation.	3rd Variation.	Air.
1—16. A.	17—35. B.	36—52. C.	53—85. D.	86. E

THIRD MOVEMENT.—"Allegro ma non Troppo," key of F minor. Sonata Form. A.

Enunciation.	Development.	Recapitulation.
1—19. Introduction. B.		212—256$^{(1)}$. 1st subject in original key. J.
20--64$^{(1)}$. 1st subject in F minor (tonic). C	118—211. H.	256—267. Connecting episode. K.
64—75. Connecting episode. D.		268—288$^{(1)}$. 2nd subject in F minor (tonic).
76—96$^{(1)}$. 2nd subject in C minor. E.		288—300. Coda. L.
96—108. Coda. F.		300—307.
108--117. G.		Double bar and repeat from bar 118.
		308—315.
		316. Coda. M.

In numbering the bars, each portion of a bar, either at the commencement or in the course of a movement, has been reckoned as one bar; the small figures in brackets denote the beat of the bar to which reference is made.

FIRST MOVEMENT.

A. The 1st subject begins with a 4-bar phrase, ending on the dominant 1$^{(4)}$-5$^{(1)}$, followed by the same phrase transposed a semitone higher, ending in D♭ major, that key being modulated to by means of the Neapolitan 6th, bars 5$^{(4)}$-7, which is also the subdominant chord of D♭ major. Bars 8-9$^{(1)}$ are repeated (in original key), bars 10-11$^{(1)}$, and at bars 12-13$^{(1)}$ in key of tonic. At bar 11$^{(3)}$ a figure is introduced undoubtedly suggestive of the principal figure of the 1st movement of Beethoven's C minor Symphony. The subject ends on half-close on the dominant, bar 17. The A♮, bar 8$^{(3)}$, should be written B♭♭, it being the minor 9th of A♭.

B. The first few bars of the connecting episode are derived from the 1st subject, bars 17$^{(4)}$-25$^{(1)}$. At bar 25 a new figure appears in triplets, forming an inverted pedal point upon the dominant of the relative major, in which key the episode ends, bar 36. The E♮ in bar 33$^{(3)}$ would be more correctly written F♭, minor 9th of dominant of A♭ major.

C. The 2nd subject, bars 36$^{(4)}$-62, is divided into two parts. The first part, bars 36-51, in A♭ major, bears some resemblance to the figure used at the commencement of the 1st subject. The last 4 bars, 48-51, lead to the key of A♭ minor, in which key the second part of this subject begins, and ends, bars 52-62; it forms a complete contrast to the previous part.

D. The development, bars 66[4]-136, contains references to both the 1st and 2nd subjects as well as to the connecting episode.   It begins, after an introductory bar, with the first 4 bars of the 1st subject in E major. Bars 25-32 are reproduced with slight alterations in the key of D♭, bars 94-106.   Bars 124-135[1] are entirely occupied with the chord of the minor 9th of the dominant, accompanied, bars 131[4]-135[1], by the figure which appeared, bar 11[4].

E. A pedal point accompanies the whole of the 1st subject on its re-appearance, bars 136[4]-140[1], upon the dominant, bars 140[4]-144[1] upon D♭; bars 145-152[4] upon the dominant.

F. The connecting episode, bars 152[4]-175, begins like the original one, but it is extended by 4 bars 160-165, after which it is transposed so as to end in F major (tonic major).

G. The first part of the 2nd subject appears in the tonic major key, bar 175.   The second part, bars 191-201, is in the tonic key.

H. The Coda is elongated, bar 205; it is constructed upon previous material.   The 2nd subject is referred to twice, at bar 211[4] in D♭ major, and at bar 241 in F minor.   The Coda ends with 6 bars of tonic harmony.

SECOND MOVEMENT.

A. The air consists of two sections of 8 bars (repeated), each section containing two phrases of 4 bars, ending with perfect cadence on tonic chord.   In bar 6 the E♮ should be written F♭, as the chord is evidently that of the German augmented 6th, roots E♭ and A♭.   This alteration in the notation, however, causes consecutive 5ths with the bass $\frac{F♭\ \ E♭}{B♭♭\ \ A♭}$.   In the variations the B♭♭ in this chord appears as A♮!

B. Syncopation is freely used in the 1st variation.

C. In the 2nd variation the harmony is in arpeggios.

D. The 3rd variation seems to combine the devices used in the two preceding variations—the syncopation of the 1st and the arpeggios of the 2nd, the latter appearing in demisemiquavers.   Instead of the repeat, this variation is written in full, the figures in bars 53[1]-61[1] being inverted, bars 61-69[1], and bars 69-77[1], at 77-85.

E. The original melody re-appears without repeats.   Instead of the final chord in the tonic, the 3rd inversion of the minor 9th interrupts the close of the air.   This chord is repeated preparatory to the entry of the 3rd movement in F minor.

THIRD MOVEMENT.

A. There is no break between the 2nd and 3rd movements.

B. The Introduction commences with the 3rd inversion of the dominant minor 9th.   This chord is repeated thirteen times.   A scale passage constructed upon it finally resolves on the tonic at bar 20.

C. The 1st subject may be divided into two parts.   The first part begins and ends in the tonic key, bars 20-28[1], repeated with alterations in the bass, bars 28-36[1].   The second part also begins and ends in the tonic key, bars 36-50[1], repeated (varied), bars 50-64.

D. The connecting episode is entirely founded upon the first 2 bars of the 1st subject, accompanied by the harmony of the tonic chord for 4 bars, 64-67, the dominant chord of C minor, bars 68-71, and the chord of C minor, bars 72-75.

E. Instead of being in the relative major key, the 2nd subject is in the key of C minor ; it ends on half close, bar 85, and is repeated (varied), bars 86-96[1]; ending with full close.

F. The Coda is founded on the 1st subject, and consists entirely of the harmony of the tonic and dominant of C minor.

G. Bars 108-117 form a passage leading to the development.

H. The development is principally based on previous material.   A new subject appears, bar 142, and continues to bar 158[1], when the 1st subject is again referred to.   It ends on dominant pedal point of 6 bars.

J. The first part of the 1st subject re-appears with a new variation, bars 220-228[1].   The second part re-appears unaltered, bars 228-256[1].

K. This connecting episode resembles the original one, and begins in the same key.   Bars 260-267 however, are transposed into the key of D♭ major, the subdominant chord of which is used in the beginning of the re-appearance of the 2nd subject, treated as a Neapolitan 6th in the key of F minor (tonic), in which key the 2nd subject is reproduced.

L. The Coda is the same as that in the enunciation, but it can only be looked upon as being the Coda of the recapitulation, not of the whole Movement ; for instead of being lengthened, and forming the concluding part of the Movement, as usual, bars 300-307, leading to a repetition of the development and recapitulation (which is unusual), after which, with bars 308-315, it leads to the final Coda, " Presto."

M. The final Coda begins with a new subject in two parts, both repeated and founded upon the same material.   (The first part begins in the tonic key, the 2nd in A♭ major.)   Bars 335 to the end are founded on the 1st subject.

SONATA No. 24.

Op. 78.

FIRST MOVEMENT.—"Adagio Cantabile" and "Allegro ma non Troppo," key of F$\sharp$ major. Sonata Form.

Enunciation.	Development.	Recapitulation.
1 — 4. "Adagio Cantabile." Introduction. A.	41—59. E.	59$^{(1)}$—63$^{(1)}$. 1st subject in original key. F.
5 — 9. 1st subject in F$\sharp$ major (tonic). B.		63$^{(1)}$—90$^{(1)}$. Connecting episode. G.
9$^{(1)}$.—29$^{(1)}$. Connecting episode. C.		90$^{(1)}$—98$^{(1)}$. 2nd subject in F$\sharp$ major (tonic). H.
29$^{(3)}$—37$^{(1)}$. 2nd subject in C$\sharp$ major.		98. Coda. J.
37 — 39$^{(3)}$. D.		Double bar and repeat from bar 42.
Double bar and repeat.		

SECOND MOVEMENT.—"Allegro Vivace," key of F$\sharp$ major. Rondo Form.

1st Part.	2nd Part.	3rd Part.
1 — 20$^{(1)}$. 1st subject in F$\sharp$ major (tonic). A.	51—149. F.	150—161. 1st subject in original key.
20$^{(2)}$—22$^{(1)}$. B.		161. Coda. G.
22 — 31. Episode. C.		
32 — 49$^{(1)}$. 1st subject in original key. D.		
49$^{(2)}$—51$^{(1)}$. E.		

Alternative Scheme.

1st Part.	2nd Part.	3rd Part.
1 — 43. 1st subject in F$\sharp$ major.	100—116. Connecting passage.	150—161. 1st subject in original key.
43 — 57. Connecting passage.	116—128. 2nd episode (transposition of 1st episode, F$\sharp$ major and minor).	161. Coda.
57 — 69. 1st episode, D$\sharp$ major and minor.	128—149. Connecting passage.	
69 — 88. Connecting passage.		
89—100. 1st subject in B major (curtailed).		

In numbering the bars, each portion of a bar, either at the commencement or in the course of a movement, has been reckoned as one bar; the small figures in brackets denote the beat of the bar to which reference is made.

FIRST MOVEMENT.

A. The Introduction is constructed upon tonic pedal point. It is not referred to again in the course of the movement.

B. The 1st subject only consists of two phrases of 2 bars each ; the latter one, $7^{(1)}$-$9^{(3)}$, being constructed upon tonic pedal point.

C. The connecting episode commences with a new figure; it continues in tonic key until bar 18. By means of an interrupted cadence, bars 18-19, it modulates to the key of D♯ minor, and then, bar 21, to C♯ major, in which key it ends, bar 29.

D. Bars 37-39$^{(9)}$ lead, in the first instance, to the repetition of the enunciation, and afterwards, with the addition of bar $41^{(9)}$ (omitting bar $39^{(3)}$), to the development.

E. The development principally refers to the 1st subject in the tonic minor key. and ends in the tonic major.

F. The 1st subject re-appears unaltered.

G. The connecting episode resembles that in the enunciation, extended and altered so as to end in F♯ major.

H. The 2nd subject re-appears transposed into the key of the tonic.

J. The Coda is an extension of the bars (letter D) at the end of the enunciation ; it contains reminiscences of the 1st subject. The development and the recapitulation are repeated.

SECOND MOVEMENT.

A. The 1st subject commences with the chord of the augmented 6th on the minor 6th of the scale. It is in two parts, bars 1-$12^{(1)}$ and bars $12^{(9)}$-$16^{(1)}$. The 2nd part is of quite a different character from the 1st ; it is repeated, $16^{(9)}$-$20^{(1)}$.

B. Bars $20^{(9)}$-$22^{(1)}$ modulate to C♯ major, the key of the following episode.

C. This episode is entirely constructed on one figure of two notes.

D. The 1st subject re-appears in its original key, the repetition of the 2nd part being curtailed.

E. Bars $49^{(9)}$-$51^{(1)}$ form a passage (corresponding with letter B) leading to episode.

F. The 2nd part commences with 6 bars resembling the 1st episode, the figure of which is inverted. At bar 57 a fresh episode is introduced, 2 bars in D♯ major, bars 57-$59^{(1)}$, alternating with 2 bars in D♯ minor, $59^{(9)}$-$61^{(1)}$, also 61-$63^{(1)}$ and $63^{(9)}$-$65^{(1)}$. This episode eventually ends, bar 74, on dominant 7th of C♮ major, followed by another reference to the 1st episode, bars $74^{(4)}$-88. At bars 89-$104^{(1)}$ the 1st subject re-appears in the key of B major, after which there occurs a passage (*see* letters B and E) leading to the repetition of bars $51^{(9)}$-88, slightly lengthened, with harmonic and melodic changes.

G. The Coda begins with several bars (161-174) constructed upon bar 11. After a short cadenza the movement closes with a variation (upon tonic pedal point) of the 2nd part of the 1st subject.

SONATINA No. 25.

OP. 79.

FIRST MOVEMENT.—"Presto alla Tedesca," key of G major. Sonata Form.

Enunciation.	Development.	Recapitulation.
1 — 8$^{(1)}$. 1st subject in G major (tonic). A.		124—131$^{(1)}$. 1st subject in original key.
8—24^{a}. Connecting episode. B.	53—124$^{(1)}$. E.	131—147$^{(1)}$. Connecting episode. F.
24—46$^{(1)}$. 2nd subject in D major. C.		147—169$^{(1)}$. 2nd subject in G major (tonic).
46—49. D.		169—174. G.
Double bar and repeat.		Double bar and repeat from bar 53.
		177. Coda. H.

SECOND MOVEMENT.—"Andante," key of G minor. Ternary Form.

1st Part.	2nd Part.	3rd Part.
1—8. 1st subject in G minor (tonic). A.	10—17$^{(1)}$. 2nd subject in E♭ major C.	22—29. 1st subject in original key.
9. B.		30. Coda. E.
	17—22$^{(1)}$. D.	

THIRD MOVEMENT.—"Vivace," key of G major. Rondo Form.

1st Part.	2nd Part.	3rd Part.
1—16. 1st subject in G major (tonic). A.	51$^{(1)}$—67. Episode in C major. D.	73—96. 1st subject in original key. F.
17—35. Episode. B.		97. Coda. G.
36—51$^{(1)}$. 1st subject in original key. C.	68 — 73$^{(1)}$. E.	

In numbering the bars, each portion of a bar, either at the commencement or in the course of a movement, has been reckoned as one bar; the small figures in brackets denote the beat of the bar to which reference is made.

—

FIRST MOVEMENT.

A. The 1st subject, consisting of a sentence of 8 bars, begins and ends in the tonic key, and is constructed upon tonic pedal point.

B. The connecting episode begins with a modulation to the dominant, after some arpeggios in that key it modulates to A major. The end of it overlaps the entry of the 2nd subject.

C. The second subject commences with a 4-bar phrase, 24-27, repeated, bars 28-31, the first 2 bars of which are in the key of A major. At bars 32-33 the bass of bars 28-29 is transferred from the bass to the treble. The subject ends with full close in the key of the dominant, bars 45-46$^{(1)}$.

D. Bars 46-49 form a passage, leading, in the first instance, to the repetition of the enunciation, and afterwards, with the addition of bars 51-52 (omitting bar 50), to the development.

E. The development refers principally to the 1st subject and the episode. It commences with the former in the key of E major. The first part of the latter appears at bar 100 in the key of E♭ major.

F. The connecting episode is of the same length, and is composed of the same material as the original one, but altered so as to end in D major.

G. Bars 169-174 form a passage leading, in the first instance, to the repetition of the development and recapitulation, afterwards, with bars 175-176 (omitting bars 171-174), leading to Coda.

H. The Coda is formed of reminiscences of the 1st subject, the first 4 bars of which are heard twice in the bass, repeated in the treble a note higher. The form of this movement closely resembles that of the last movement of No. 23, Op. 57.

SECOND MOVEMENT.*

A. The 1st subject consists of 2 sentences of 4 bars; the first ends in relative major key, the 2nd ends in tonic key (G minor).

B. Bar 9 modulates to the key of E♭ major

C. The 2nd subject, which does not modulate, begins and ends in the key of E♭ major.

D. Bars 17-22$^{(1)}$ form a passage leading back to the tonic key.

E. The Coda is derived from the 1st subject.

THIRD MOVEMENT.

A. The 1st subject is divided into two parts; the first part, bars 1-8, ending in dominant key; the second part, bars 9-16, beginning in dominant and ending in tonic key. Both parts are repeated.

B. This episode consists of an 8-bar sentence, 17$^{(1)}$-25$^{(1)}$, in E minor, followed by several bars formed upon the 1st subject, modulating back to tonic key.

C. The 1st subject re-appears with a varied accompaniment; the repetition is omitted.

D. This episode commences with a 4-bar phrase, 51$^{(1)}$-55$^{(1)}$, repeated a fourth higher, 55$^{(1)}$-59$^{(1)}$. Bars 59$^{(1)}$-67$^{(1)}$ are a varied repetition of bars 51$^{(1)}$-59$^{(1)}$.

E. Bars 68-73$^{(1)}$ form a passage leading to third entry of 1st subject.

F. The first part of the 1st subject, bars 73-80 (which re-appears here with a new accompaniment), is repeated with considerable variation, bars 81-88.

G. The Coda is entirely formed upon the 1st subject.

* For an interesting analysis of the rhythmic construction of this movement, *see* par. 355, "Musical Form," Ebenezer Prout.

SONATA No. 26.

Op. 81a. "Sonate Caracteristique, Les Adieux, l'Absence, et le Retour." **A.**

FIRST MOVEMENT.—"Les Adieux." "Adagio," key of E♭ major. B. Introduction (bars 1—16) to "Allegro." "Allegro," key of E♭ major. Sonata Form.

Enunciation.	Development.	Recapitulation.
1 — 9[1]. 1st subject in E♭ major (tonic). C.		96—104. 1st subject in original key. J.
9 — 34[1]. Connecting episode. D.	56—95. H.	104—128[1]. Connecting episode. K.
34 — 42. 2nd subject in B♭ major. E.		128—136. 2nd subject in E♭ major (tonic).
42 — 49. Coda. F.		
49[1]—55. G.		136. Coda. L.
Double bar and repeat.		

SECOND MOVEMENT.—"L'Absence." "Andante Espressivo," key of C minor. Modified Sonata Form. **A.**

Enunciation.	Development.	Recapitulation.
1 — 8[1]. 1st subject in G minor and C minor (tonic). B.		21 — 24.[1] 1st subject in F minor. G.
8[1]—14. Connecting episode. C.	None. F.	24[1]—30. Connecting episode. H.
15 — 19. 2nd subject in G major. D.		31 — 35[1]. 2nd subject in F major. J.
19 — 20. E.		35 — 42. K.

THIRD MOVEMENT.—"Le Retour." "Vivacissimamente," key of E♭ major. Sonata Form.

1—10. Introduction. A.

Enunciation.	Development.	Recapitulation.
11 — 29[1]. 1st subject in E♭ major (tonic). B.		110[1]—123[1]. 1st subject in original key. F.
29 — 52[1]. Connecting episode. C.	82[1]—110. E.	123 — 146[1]. Connecting episode. G.
52[1]—81. 2nd subject in B flat major. D.		146[1]—177[1]. 2nd subject in E♭ major (tonic). H.
Double bar and repeat from bar 11.		177[1]. Coda. J.

In numbering the bars, each portion of a bar, either at the commencement or in the course of a movement, has been reckoned as one bar; the small figures in brackets denote the beat of the bar to which reference is made.

FIRST MOVEMENT.

A. This is the only Piano Sonata to which Beethoven has affixed a title to indicate its contents.

B. The introduction forms the foundation of a great deal of the succeeding movement, the first three notes ("Lebe-wohl") especially being used in various forms in the 1st subject and connecting episode, at the commencement of the 2nd subject, in the development, and in the Coda. The first six bars are repeated, bars 7-12, slightly altered and transposed.

C. The 1st subject commences upon the subdominant chord, which is followed by a sequence, bars $1^{(4)}$-2 formed upon the "Lebe-wohl" phrase. The figure of the variation of it is evidently taken from bars $2^{(4)}$-$3^{(1)}$ of introduction. The "Lebe-wohl" phrase occurs in the bass with the first note dotted, bars 3-4$^{(1)}$. These first 4 bars at first sight seem to be a continuation of the introduction, but they evidently form part of the 1st subject, which is in two sections, bars 1-5$^{(1)}$ and $5^{(8)}$-$9^{(1)}$.

D. The connecting episode begins with a repetition of the 2nd section of the 1st subject followed by some passages in contrary motion. The "Lebe-wohl" phrase then appears, bars 19-22, in the bass and (inverted) in the treble, in the same form as in the bass of bars 3-4$^{(1)}$; it also occurs in the treble, bars $30^{(4)}$-$32^{(1)}$, the first note being prolonged. The episode ends with full close in the key of the dominant.

E. The second subject begins with the "Lebe-wohl" phrase augmented (quadrupled). Bars 34-37 are repeated, bars 38-41, an octave lower.

F. The first two bars of the Coda are repeated, bars 44-45, an octave higher. Bars 46-49 are based upon the "Lebe-wohl" phrase treated in various ways (by diminution in the treble, bar 46).

G. Bars 49-55 form a passage suggestive of the "Lebe-wohl" phrase, bars 49-53, leading to the repetition of the enunciation, bars $49^{(4)}$-51 and 54-55, leading to the development.

H. The development commences with a reference to the beginning of the 1st subject, which, with the "Lebe-wohl" phrase, forms the chief material on which it is based.

J. The 1st subject re-appears unaltered.

K. The connecting episode is of nearly the same length and character as before (bar 15 being omitted), it is altered to end in tonic key.

L. The Coda, with the exception of bars 148-166, which contain a reference to the 1st subject, is almost entirely based upon the "Lebe-wohl" phrase, which appears in different forms that are easily traceable. In single notes, bars 167-176; in thirds, bars 177-181, accompanied by a passage in semi-quavers, first below and afterwards above it, bars 183-208; in canon at the octave below, bars 209-224, diminished, bars 221-224; and lastly at bar 229 on inverted pedal point.

SECOND MOVEMENT.

A. This movement, though following the outlines of Sonata form, is very irregular.

B. The 1st subject, instead of being in the tonic key, begins with two bars in G minor, followed by two bars in G major, the same four bars are then repeated in C minor (tonic).

C. The connecting episode commences in the key of A♭ major, modulating to F minor, bars 9-10. A reference to the 1st subject in G minor is succeeded by a scale passage leading to the 2nd subject.

D. The second subject, instead of being in the relative major, is in the key of the dominant major.

E. Bars 19-20 lead to the re-entry of the 1st subject.

F. There is no development in this movement.

G. The 1st subject re-appears in F minor instead of tonic key.

H. The connecting episode is similar to the original one, altered so as to lead to the key of F major.

J. The 2nd subject, instead of being in the tonic key, re-appears here in F major.

K. Bars 35-42 form a passage leading to the next movement, there being no break between the 2nd and 3rd movements.

THIRD MOVEMENT.

A. This introduction is entirely formed of arpeggios on dominant harmony.

B. The 1st subject is divided into three sections overlapping each other, and each beginning and ending in tonic key. The first, bars 11-17, with subject in the treble; the 2nd, bars 17-23, with subject in the bass accompanied by a new figure in the treble; the third, bars 23-29$^{(1)}$, with the subject still in the bass, but with a different accompaniment in the treble.

C. The connecting episode begins with florid passages upon tonic pedal point (bars 29-36). At bars 36-37 there is a modulation to the dominant. Bars 37-40 constitute a 4-bar phrase in G♭ major, repeated, bars 41-44, in F major; bars 37-44 being repeated, bars 45-52, with additions and variations. Bars 37-40 and 45-48 in G♭ major are evidently formed upon the chord of the Neapolitan 6th in the key of F, the dominant of the key of the second subject.

D. The second subject may be divided into 4 bar phrases throughout. The 1st phrase, bars 53-56, is repeated, bars 61-64, an octave higher. The second phrase, bars 57-60, is repeated, bars 65-68, varied and inverted. Bars 69-70 are repeated, 71-72, an octave lower; bars 73-74 are repeated, 75-76, slightly altered, an octave lower. It ends with a species of Coda of 4 bars, tonic and dominant harmony, in the key of the dominant.

E. The development begins with new material, after which, bar 95, the 2nd subject appears in B major, first in the bass and then in the treble. At bar 105 there is a reference to the 1st subject, leading to its re-appearance.

F. The 1st subject re-appears with a different accompaniment, and on its repetition in the bass 116⁽⁸⁾-123⁽¹⁾, the accompaniment is again new (the second repetition is omitted).

G. The connecting episode is identical with that in the enunciation, altered so as to lead to the tonic key instead of the dominant.

H. The second subject is elongated by 2 bars (171-172), otherwise it is literally transposed into tonic key.

J. The Coda, " Poco Andante," is formed upon the first subject.

SONATA No. 27.

Op. 90.

FIRST MOVEMENT.—Key of E minor. Sonata Form.

Enunciation.	Development.	Recapitulation.
1 — 25⁽¹⁾. 1st subject in E minor (tonic). A.		144⁽⁸⁾—168⁽¹⁾. 1st subject in original key. E.
25⁽⁸⁾—55. Connecting episode. B.	83—144⁽⁷⁾. D.	168⁽³⁾—198. Connecting episode. F.
56 — 68. 2nd subject in B minor. C.		199 — 211. 2nd subject in E minor (tonic). G.
68 — 82. Coda.		211. Coda. H.

SECOND MOVEMENT.—Key of E major. Rondo Form.

1st Part.	2nd Part.	3rd Part.
1 — 33⁽⁸⁾. 1st subject in E major (tonic). A.		140⁽⁴⁾—172⁽⁸⁾. 1st subject in original key. F.
33⁽⁴⁾— 41⁽¹⁾. Episode. B.	102⁽⁴⁾—140. Development. E.	172⁽⁸⁾—181⁽¹⁾. Episode. G.
41⁽⁸⁾— 70. 2nd subject in B major. C.		181⁽²⁾—230. 2nd subject in E major (tonic). H.
70⁽⁴⁾—102⁽¹⁾. 1st subject in original key. D.		230⁽⁴⁾—254⁽¹⁾. 1st subject in original key. J.
		254⁽²⁾. Coda. K.

In numbering the bars, each portion of a bar, either at the commencement or in the course of a movement, has been reckoned as one bar; the small figures in brackets denote the beat of the bar to which reference is made.

FIRST MOVEMENT.

A. Very little of the 1st subject is in the key of the tonic. The first phrase commencing in tonic key and modulating to G major, bars 1-5$^{(1)}$, is repeated (beginning in the key of G major and ending in B minor), bars 5$^{(0)}$-9$^{(1)}$. The second phrase, bars 9$^{(2)}$-17, begins in G major and ends with a pause on the dominant chord of E minor (tonic), succeeded by a 4-bar phrase in that key, 17$^{(0)}$-21$^{(2)}$, which is repeated, bars 21$^{(3)}$-25$^{(1)}$, ending with full close on tonic. Excepting the slight reference to the relative major key in the 1st subject, none of the movement is in that key.

B. The connecting episode commences in tonic key, bars 25$^{(2)}$-29$^{(1)}$. A 4-bar passage, 29$^{(2)}$-33$^{(1)}$, in the key of C major is repeated, 33$^{(0)}$-37$^{(1)}$, in A minor. A part of the same passage in B♭ major is followed by a modulation to B minor upon the dominant minor 9th of which it leads into the 2nd subject.

C. The 2nd subject (instead of being in the relative major) is in B minor. Bars 56-61 are repeated (varied), 62-67.

D. The development (preluded by a repetition of the three notes at the end of the 2nd subject) commences with a reference to the first phrase of 1st subject. At bar 102 some new material is introduced, consisting of a chromatic passage which leads to a development of the second phrase of the 1st subject. The development ends, bar 144, in tonic key.

E. The 1st subject re-appears in its original state.

F. The connecting episode is composed of the same material as in the enunciation, transposed so as to end in tonic key.

G. The 2nd subject is transposed into the tonic key without any alteration.

H. The Coda is elongated, bar 223.

SECOND MOVEMENT.

A. The 1st subject begins with a 4-bar section, 1$^{(0)}$-5$^{(0)}$, repeated (in octaves) 5$^{(0)}$-9$^{(1)}$, followed by an 8-bar section commencing in the dominant key, modulating to A major and ending in tonic key, 9$^{(2)}$-17$^{(1)}$, repeated (in octaves), 17$^{(0)}$-25$^{(1)}$. The 1st subject ends with the first section and its repetition (varied), bars 25$^{(2)}$-33$^{(0)}$.

B. Bars 33$^{(2)}$-41$^{(1)}$ form an episode (based upon bars 9$^{(0)}$-11$^{(1)}$) leading to the key of the dominant.

C. The 2nd subject may be divided into 2 parts. The first part, 41$^{(2)}$-61$^{(0)}$, is constructed almost entirely upon inverted dominant pedal point of B major. Bars 41$^{(2)}$-46$^{(1)}$ are repeated (varied), bars 49$^{(2)}$-54$^{(1)}$. The second part, bars 61-70, consists of a 4-bar phrase in B major (61-64), repeated (65-68) in tonic key, leading with two additional bars to the second entry of the 1st subject. Alternative scheme: 2nd subject, bars 41-61; connecting episode, bars 61-70.

D. The 1st subject re-appears unaltered.

E. The development commences with a passage based upon the last 5 notes of the 1st subject, leading to several repetitions of the second part of the 2nd subject in C major, C minor, C♯ minor, and C♯ major. A passage built upon the chord of the dominant minor ninth leads to the third entry of the 1st subject.

F. The 1st subject re-appears unaltered.

G. Bars 172$^{(0)}$-181$^{(1)}$ form a passage similar to 33$^{(0)}$-41$^{(1)}$ altered so as to end in tonic key.

H. The 2nd subject, which is transposed to tonic key, is extended at bar 210 by a passage which introduces some development of bars 3$^{(0)}$-5. At bar 222 it ends with a passage based upon dominant harmony in canon, bars 222$^{(2)}$-230.

J. The 1st subject is considerably varied, both the first and second sections appearing with the melody in an inner part, accompanied by a semiquaver figure in the treble, bars 230$^{(0)}$-234$^{(1)}$ and bars 238$^{(0)}$-246$^{(0)}$. The repetition of the first part of the 1st subject is omitted.

K. The Coda is formed on previous matter, the first section of the 1st subject appearing at bar 276$^{(4)}$.

(55)

SONATA No. 28.

Op. 101.

FIRST MOVEMENT.—"Allegretto ma non Troppo," key of A major. Sonata Form.

Enunciation.	Development.	Recapitulation.
1 — 4. 1st subject in A major (tonic). A.		55 — 57. 1st subject (shortened) in original key. F.
5 — 16$^{(1)}$. Connecting episode. B.	35—55. E.	
16$^{(4)}$—25. 2nd subject in E major. C.		58 — 68. Connecting episode. G.
25 — 33$^{(1)}$. Coda. D.		68$^{(4)}$—77. 2nd subject in A major (tonic). H.
		77. Coda. J.

SECOND MOVEMENT.—"Vivace alla Marcia." Ternary Form. A.

Key of F major.	Key of B♭ major.	
1st Part. B.	2nd Part. H.	3rd Part.
1 — 9. 1st subject in F major, (tonic), C ending in C major (dominant).	58 — 60. J.	Marcia.
Double bar and repeat.	61 — 63. 1st subject in B♭ major (tonic). K.	(1st Part)
10$^{(3)}$—13. Coda, ending in tonic key. D.	64 — 69$^{(1)}$. 2nd subject in F major (dominant). L.	Da Capo.
14 — 37. Development. E.	69$^{(1)}$—80$^{(1)}$. Development. M.	
37 — 42. 1st subject. F.	80 — 82. 1st subject in original key. N.	
Double bar and repeat.	83 — 88. 2nd subject in B♭ major (tonic). O.	
42$^{(3)}$—57. Coda. G.	88 — 98. P.	

INTRODUCTION TO THIRD MOVEMENT.—"Adagio ma non Troppo, con Affetto," key of A minor, 1—20. A. "Tempo del Primo Pezzo," key of A major, 1—8. B.

THIRD MOVEMENT.—"Allegro," key of A major. Sonata Form.

Enunciation.	Development.	Recapitulation.
1 — 4. Introduction. C.	96—204$^{(3)}$. In Fugue Form. J.	204$^{(4)}$—225. 1st subject in original key. K.
4$^{(4)}$—37$^{(1)}$. 1st subject in A major (tonic). D.		225 — 252. Connecting episode. L.
37 —62$^{(3)}$. Connecting episode. E.		252$^{(4)}$—260. 2nd subject in A major (tonic). M.
62$^{(4)}$—70. 2nd subject in E major. F.		260. Coda. N.
Double bar and repeat.		
70 — 85. Coda. G.		
86$^{(4)}$—95. H.		
Double bar and repeat from bar 4.		

In numbering the bars, each portion of a bar, either at the commencement or in the course of a movement, has been reckoned as one bar; the small figures in brackets denote the beat of the bar to which reference is made.

FIRST MOVEMENT.

A. The 1st subject consists of only 4 bars, 1-4, beginning and ending upon the dominant. Note the appearance of the 1st subject in the introduction to the finale.

B. The connecting episode begins with a repetition of the first 2 bars of the 1st subject, after which it is in the dominant key throughout; the initial figure of the 2nd subject is foreshadowed, beginning bar 9. It ends with interrupted cadence.

C. The 2nd subject, which is like a continuation of the episode, commences with a 4-bar phrase 16$^{(4)}$-20$^{(1)}$, followed by a 5-bar phrase, 20$^{(3)}$-25$^{(1)}$. Out of the 9 bars forming the 2nd subject, 6 of them, 19-25, are constructed entirely upon tonic and dominant harmony of E major.

D. The Coda begins with 4 bars of tonic and dominant harmony of E major, after which there is a double pedal point.

E. The development, after 2 bars of the chord of the dominant, commences with several references to the 1st subject, bars 35-42, after which the first three notes of bar 2 are considerably developed.

F. Only a fragment of the 1st subject re-appears here, and this is varied and transposed to tonic minor key.

G. The original connecting episode is altered, bars $59^{(4)}$-60, but bars $60^{(4)}$-$68^{(1)}$ are the same as bars $8^{(4)}$-$16^{(1)}$, slightly varied, and transposed into tonic key.

H. The 2nd subject (transposed into tonic key) is slightly altered at bar 76, probably because of the limited compass of the keyboard in Beethoven's time.

J. The Coda is elongated at bar 85. At bars $98^{(4)}$-$99^{(1)}$ there is a reference to the 2nd subject, which is inverted, bars $99^{(4)}$-$100^{(1)}$.

SECOND MOVEMENT.

A. This movement evidently takes the place of the Scherzo.

B. The first part is in simple Binary Form. The bass of bars 1-8 proceeds chromatically (though not in the same octave) from F down to F$\sharp$ (with the exception of B$\natural$).

C. The 1st subject (which is repeated) modulates to, and ends in, the dominant.

D. Bar 9 is repeated at bar 11 (an octave higher) and at bar 12-13 in the key of F (tonic).

E. The development commences with a figure from bars 2-3 used in imitation. At bars 17-19 a new figure is introduced, imitated in the bass, bars 18-20. The rest of the development consists of references to the 1st subject.

F. Only the 2nd part of the 1st subject is repeated (varied) upon dominant pedal.

G. The Coda begins with a vigorous passage of imitation founded upon bar 5. After several passages in contrary motion, the end of the first subject, which originally appeared in the dominant key, occurs transposed into tonic key, bars 54-56.

H. The 2nd part is in simple Binary Form.

J. Bars 58-60 form an introduction to the 2nd part.

K. The 1st subject only consists of 2 bars, 61-62, bar 63 being an inversion of bar 62.

L. The 2nd subject is in canon at the octave below, it begins and ends in dominant key.

M. The development, which overlaps the 2nd subject, is also in canon at the octave throughout, leading off with a subject taken from the bass of bars 62-63, which gives place to a new figure at bar 74.

N. The 1st subject re-appears, accompanied by pedal point in the treble.

O. The antecedent of the canon constituting the 2nd subject re-appears here in the bass instead of in the treble as originally.

P. Bars 88-98 form a passage which leads to the repetition of part 1. Bars 88-94 are founded upon the rhythm of bars 59-60. Bars 95-98 are almost an exact repetition of 38-41, upon dominant pedal of F throughout.

THIRD MOVEMENT.

A. This Adagio may be looked upon as a distinct slow movement, but it is evidently an introduction to the finale, being fragmentary in character. It begins with dominant harmony and is for the most part constructed upon the figure in the treble of bar 1. It ends at bar 20 with a cadenza upon dominant chord.

B. The 1st subject of the 1st movement re-appears in its original key, the 2 phrases of which it is composed being separated by a pause ; the last three notes of bar 4 are repeated at different intervals, bars 5-7. At bar 8 the time changes to Presto.

C. Bars 1-4 upon dominant harmony lead to the 1st subject of the finale.

D. The 1st subject is of considerable length, and may be divided into 2 parts. The first part, bars $4^{(4)}$-$20^{(3)}$: the whole movement is constructed mainly upon the initial figure. The first 8 bars, $4^{(4)}$-$12^{(3)}$, are repeated (inverted and altered to end in tonic key), bars $12^{(4)}$-$20^{(3)}$. The 2nd part, bars $20^{(4)}$-$29^{(1)}$, begins with a new figure in the treble, bars $20^{(4)}$-$22^{(3)}$, repeated in an inner part, bars $22^{(4)}$-$24^{(3)}$; the remaining bars of the 2nd part, $24^{(4)}$-$29^{(1)}$, are constructed on bars $20^{(4)}$-$21^{(3)}$, and lead to the resumption of the 1st part (inverted), the conclusion of which is treated canonically at the octave. The 1st subject ends with full close, bar $37^{(1)}$.

E. The connecting episode is in 2 distinct parts, the semiquaver figure of the 1st part, bars 37-$52^{(3)}$, is taken from bar 5. The first part begins in tonic key and modulates to E major, upon the dominant 7th of which key it ends, bar $52^{(3)}$. The 2nd part consists of two phrases quite distinct from the preceding material ; the 1st phrase of 6 bars' length, $53^{(3)}$-$59^{(1)}$, and the 2nd phrase consisting of 4 bars, $59^{(3)}$-$62^{(3)}$, in the key of E major.

F. The 2nd subject is clearly taken from the beginning of the 1st subject, it is imitated by an inner part at the 5th.

G. The Coda mainly consists of a figure in the bass, bars 70-71, imitated in the treble, bars 72-73.

H. Bars $86^{(4)}$-95 form a passage leading to the development.

J. The development is in fugue form, which is unusual. The subject of it (which is taken from the 1st subject) begins in A minor, bars $96^{(4)}$-103. The answer appears, $103^{(4)}$-110, accompanied by a counter-subject. The subject then re-appears, bars $110^{(4)}$-$117^{(3)}$; the last part of it is imitated by an inner part at the under 9th. The subject occurs again at bars $118^{(4)}$-125 ; at bars $128^{(1)}$-134. Note the consecutive 5ths, bar 125. An episode formed upon a fragment of the subject, bars 134-$141^{(3)}$, is succeeded by one based upon the initial figure of the subject, bars $141^{(4)}$-$145^{(4)}$. The subject appears again in the key of C, bars 145"-152. Another episode of considerable length leads to tne stretto, bars 181-187. Aftet a canonical reference to the subject, the fugue ends upon dominant pedal point; 4 bars of arpeggios on the dominant chord lead to the recapitulation.

K. The 1st subject is shortened on its re-appearance here ; it proceeds as before for 8 bars, after which (upon inverted dominant pedal, bars 212$^{(6)}$-216), the initial figure appears direct in the bass and inverted in the treble, imitated a bar's length at the octave in an inner part. A somewhat new treatment of the passage, beginning bar 32, leads to the connecting episode.

L. The 1st part of the connecting episode, with some harmonic and melodic changes, resembles the original one ; the 2nd part is identical, transposed a 4th higher, ending in tonic key.

M. The 2nd subject (with slight alterations) is transposed into tonic key.

N. The Coda is built upon previous material ; at bar 276 it is elongated, at bar 279 it refers to the 1st subject, followed, at bar 298, by the 2nd part of 1st subject, bars 20$^{(6)}$-29$^{(1)}$ (which is omitted in the recapitulation). The movement ends with tonic pedal point, bar 320 to the end.

SONATA No. 29.

Op. 106.

FIRST MOVEMENT.—"Allegro," key of B♭ major. Sonata Form.

Enunciation.	Development.	Recapitulation.
1 — 18$^{(1)}$. 1st subject in B♭ major (tonic). A.	131—233. G.	233$^{(6)}$—256$^{(1)}$. 1st subject in original key. H.
18 — 64$^{(1)}$. Connecting episode. B.		256 — 302 . Connecting episode. J.
63$^{(6)}$—101$^{(1)}$. 2nd subject in G major. C.		301$^{(6)}$—339$^{(1)}$. 2nd subject in B♭ major (tonic). K.
101 — 121$^{(1)}$. Coda. D.		339. Coda. L.
121 — 126. E.		
Double bar and repeat.		
127 — 130. F.		

SECOND MOVEMENT.—"Scherzo," "Assai Vivace," key of B♭ major. Ternary Form.

1st Part.	2nd Part.	3rd Part.
1—47. 1st subject in B♭ major (tonic). A.	47 — 98$^{(1)}$. 2nd subject in B♭ minor. B.	116—162$^{(6)}$. 1st subject in original key. D.
	98—115. C.	162. Coda. E.

THIRD MOVEMENT.—"Adagio Sostenuto," key of F♯ minor. Sonata Form.

Enunciation.	Development.	Recapitulation.
2 — 27$^{(1)}$. 1st subject in F♯ minor (tonic). A.	69—88$^{(1)}$. E.	88 — 112. 1st subject (varied) in original key. F.
27 — 45$^{(1)}$. Connecting episode. B.		113 — 130$^{(1)}$. Connecting episode. G.
45 — 63$^{(1)}$. 2nd subject in D major. C.		130 — 148 . 2nd subject in F♯ major (tonic). H.
63$^{(6)}$—69$^{(1)}$. Coda. D.		148$^{(6)}$. Coda. J.

FOURTH MOVEMENT.—A. Introduction, "Largo," "Allegro," "Prestissimo," and bars 1—5$^{(1)}$ of "Allegro Risoluto."

Allegro Risoluto, key of B♭ major. B. Rondo and Fugue Form (combined).

1st Part.	2nd Part.	3rd Part.
6 — 84. 1st subject and episodes in B♭ major (tonic). C.	106$^{(6)}$—186. Development and episode. E.	186$^{(6)}$—269$^{(6)}$. 1st subject and episodes in D major. F.
84$^{(6)}$—106$^{(6)}$. 1st subject in E♭ minor. D.		269$^{(6)}$—356. 1st subject in B♭ major (tonic). G.
		357. Coda. H.

In numbering the bars, each portion of a bar, either at the commencement or in the course of a movement, has been reckoned as one bar ; the small figures in brackets denote the beat of the bar to which reference is made.

FIRST MOVEMENT.

A. The 1st subject is in two sections ; the first section, bars 1-$5^{(1)}$; the second section, bars $5^{(1)}$-$9^{(2)}$, ending on dominant ; the latter section is repeated and elongated, ending with full close on tonic.

B. The connecting episode commences with a subject of 2 bars, which is repeated three times with different harmony, bars 18-25. A passage closely following, beginning in octaves and ending on the dominant, prepares the ear for a reference to the first phrase of the 1st subject, the rhythm of which is used for a modulation to D major, bars $37^{(4)}$-$39^{(1)}$. Bars $39^{(4)}$-$46^{(1)}$ are formed upon the dominant chord of G major, in the key of which an episode follows, which leads to the 2nd subject, bars $46^{(2)}$-$64^{(1)}$.

C. The 2nd subject begins with the melody in an inner part. (Note that the concluding 3 notes of the bass of the preceding episode (bars $63^{(4)}$-$64^{(1)}$) also form the 3 first notes of the 2nd subject, bars $63^{(4)}$-$64^{(1)}$). Bars $63^{(4)}$-$67^{(2)}$ are repeated, bars $67^{(2)}$-$71^{(2)}$, altered to end in E minor. A sequential passage modulating into D minor, C major, B minor, A major, and G major, bars $71^{(4)}$-75, leads to 2 bars in the latter key (repeated) followed by 2 bars modulating to D major. These six bars are repeated in different octaves, bars 82-87, and followed by a sequential passage, bars 88-91, leading to a modulation to C major (where a new figure is introduced, $92^{(2)}$-$93^{(2)}$). This soon gives place to 4 bars in the key of G, which end the 2nd subject.

D. The Coda begins with a new subject of 6 bars, repeated (varied), bars 107-112. A passage beginning with the dominant 7th of C major brings the first part to an end in G major (bar $121^{(1)}$).

E. Bars 121-126, passage leading to the repetition of the enunciation.

F. Bars 127-130 form a passage leading to the development.

G. The development begins with a passage suggestive of the commencement of the connecting episode ending in E♭ major, bars 131-138. Five bars (139-143), in the same key, are followed by a fugal treatment of a subject, which is considerably developed (bars $144^{(4)}$-$148^{(1)}$)—the first part founded upon bars 1-3, the latter part suggested by the first 3 notes of the 2nd subject. At bars $183^{(4)}$-187 a passage occurs which is repeated in different keys, bars 188-195. At bar 208 there is a reference to the Coda, bar 101. At bar $219^{(4)}$ the fugal treatment of the first part of the 1st subject occurs again, forming a passage leading to the second entry of the 1st subject.

H. The 1st subject re-appears considerably altered. The beginning of it is accompanied by a figure, the rhythm of which may be found, among other places, at the commencement of the 2nd subject. The succeeding bars are differently harmonised as far as the pause (bar 241), and the latter part, instead of ending in the tonic key as before, is elongated, and closes in G♭ major.

J. The connecting episode is constructed on much the same material as in the enunciation, transposed into different keys. It begins in G♭ major and ends in tonic key.

K. The 2nd subject re-appears transposed, to begin and end in tonic key.

L. Bars 339-358 of the Coda resemble that in the enunciation transposed so as to begin and end in tonic key. Bar 357 is then developed to bar 369, where there is a reference to the commencement of the original Coda. A scale passage, bars 380-383, leads to some new material. The Coda ends with reminiscences of the 1st subject.

SECOND MOVEMENT.

A. Nearly the whole of the first part is constructed upon bars 1-$2^{(1)}$. The first 8 bars ending on dominant are repeated an octave higher, slightly altered. Some development follows, bars $15^{(4)}$-31. which bars are also repeated with slight variation, $31^{(4)}$-47.

B. The second part commences with a passage beginning in B♭ minor, ending in D♭ major, bars 47-55, which is repeated with the parts inverted, bars 55$^{(4)}$-63$^{(1)}$. The same passage then appears, bars 64$^{(4)}$-72$^{(1)}$, beginning in D♭ major, ending in B♭ minor (the keys being reversed). It occurs again bars 72$^{(4)}$-80$^{(1)}$, with the parts reversed. After 2 bars in B♭ minor, 80-81, the time changes to Presto, and a new subject is introduced, bars 82-89, beginning in B♭ minor, and ending in F major, repeated (varied), bars 90-97$^{(1)}$, beginning in F major and ending in B♭ minor.

C. Bars 98-115 form a passage, the commencement of which is founded on " Presto," leading to the repetition of part 1.

D. Part 1 is repeated in its entirety.

E. The Coda commences with a modulation to B minor by enharmonic change, B♭-A♯. It closes with a reference to the commencement of part 1.

THIRD MOVEMENT.

A. The 1st subject is preceded by an introductory bar (1). At bars 14-15 there is a curious modulation to G major ; bars 10-17 are repeated (varied and extended), bars 18-26.

B. The connecting episode commences, after one bar of introduction, with a new syncopated subject of 3 bars (28-31$^{(1)}$), repeated (varied), bars 31-34$^{(1)}$. Bar 34 is repeated (varied), 35, after which a passage follows modulating to D major, bars 36-45$^{(1)}$.

C. The 2nd subject leads off with a phrase, the melody of which is in the bass, bars 45-46 (the notes forming it simply consisting of the triad of D major), repeated in the treble, bars 47-48. The same phrase (varied) then occurs in the bass, with semiquaver triplet accompaniment, bars 49-50, and is repeated again in the treble, with the same accompaniment, bars 51-52, followed by an ascending passage in the treble (bars 53$^{(4)}$-56) of 4 bars (accompanied by semiquaver figure), the bass being 2 octaves and a 3rd below it until bar 56, where it is a 10th below. The 2nd subject ultimately ends with full close in D major, bars 62$^{(4)}$-63$^{(1)}$.

D. The Coda simply confirms the final cadence of the 2nd subject ; it ends on the chord of the 6th, bar 69$^{(1)}$.

E. The development begins in D major with a varied repetition of the first 3 bars of the 1st subject (bars 69-71), which is repeated in the bass in F♯ minor, bars 73-75. The first bar of the 1st subject occurs at bar 77 in E♭ major, after which the whole of the development is based upon the outline of the first 4 notes of the 1st subject, which form a triad, beginning, bar 78, with C♭, A♭, F, and followed by D♭, B♭, G— D♯, B♮, G♯—E, C♯, A♯, &c., ending with a cadenza upon dominant 9th of the tonic (bar 87).

F. The 1st subject re-appears considerably varied throughout.

G. The connecting episode begins in D major, and, though it resembles that in the enunciation, it is considerably altered so as to end in the tonic major key. The original connecting episode commenced in F♯ minor (tonic), and ended in D major; this one begins in D major and ends in F♯ major.

H. The 2nd subject appears, varied, and transposed into tonic major key.

J. The Coda commences as in the enunciation (the key being changed from D to F♯ major), and refers to both the 1st and 2nd subjects. The key signature changes to 1 sharp, bar 156; 2 sharps, bar 164 ; and to 3 sharps, bar 166. From this bar to the end, the Coda is based upon the 1st subject in tonic key. It ends, however, with the major tonic chord. (*Tierce de Picardie.*)

FOURTH MOVEMENT.

A. This introduction is very fragmentary in character, and is not in any prescribed form. It is divided into 4 parts, each forming a totally different subject; part 1 beginning in F major, "Largo," ending on chord of B major; part 2 ("un poco piu vivace"), beginning and ending in B major; part 3 ("Allegro"), beginning and ending in G♯ minor; part 4 (bars 9 to bar 5 of the "Allegro Risoluto"), beginning in A major and ending in B♭ major, the tonic A being used as leading note to B♭. A continuation of the introduction overlaps the entry of the 1st subject, bar 6. Between parts 2 and 3 (end of bar 2), also parts 3 and 4 (bar 8), there is a reference to part 1.

B. This is the 1st movement (taking these Sonatas in the order in which they were published) containing a combination of forms. Some writers consider this movement in Fugue Form.

C. The 1st subject consists of a passage, bars 6-13[1], treated fugally at considerable length. After a short codetta it is answered tonally, bars 16-23[1], the last 2 notes being altered. A counter-subject appears at bars 17-22. The subject enters again in tonic key in the bass (slightly shortened) at bar 25, and the counter-subject at bar 26 in the treble. An episode, bars 32-55, formed upon the subject and counter-subject and codetta leads to the entry of the subject in the treble in A♭ major, bar 55. Another episode, formed upon the end of the subject and a part of the counter-subject (partly in double counterpoint), closes in G♭ major, bar 75[1], followed by a series of imitations beginning in G♭ major and ending in E♭ minor (principally based upon the figure in bar 75), which lead to the re-entry of the 1st subject.

D. The 1st subject, instead of re-appearing in tonic key (which it usually does at the end of Part I. in a Rondo), enters in E♭ minor (augmented), answered (partially) at bar 101 in the treble, and at bar 102, by inversion in the bass. The 1st part ends in D♭ major, bar 106[1].

E. The development refers, from bar 106[1] to 142, principally, to previous material. At bar 143 a new subject is introduced in B minor, followed by further development of fragments of the 1st subject.

F. The subject re-appears, bar 186 (slightly shortened), in D major in the bass, answered by inversion in G major, bar 198, and slightly altered (also by inversion) at bar 206 in an inner part. An episode formed mainly upon the subject, ending bar 239 on the chord of A major, is followed by a new episode in D major—it is imitatory in character.

G. The subject re-appears (shortened) in various parts, commencing bar 269 in tonic, the beginning of the episode (bar 240) being combined with it. It is answered in the key of the dominant (inverted), bar 284[2], in the bass, and direct, bar 284[3], in the treble. The subject enters again, bar 290[2] (inverted), in the treble, and at bar 290[4] direct in the bass. The rest of this section of the movement is occupied with references to previous material, which is introduced in almost every conceivable form of imitation. It ends with full close in tonic key, bar 356.

H. The chief feature of the Coda is the pedal point which commences, bar 359[2], on the subdominant (E♭) proceeding to the dominant, bar 362[3], upon which a tonic pedal point is added. This double pedal point continues to bar 371. The whole of the Coda is founded upon the 1st subject and counter-subject. It ends with full close in tonic key.

SONATA No. 30

Op. 109.

FIRST MOVEMENT.—"Vivace ma non Troppo," key of E major. Rondo Form.

1st Part.	2nd Part.	3rd Part.
1 — 9. 1st subject in E major (tonic). A.		68—89[1]. 1st subject (varied), in original key. E.
10—16. Episode. B.	60—67. Episode. D.	
17—59. 1st subject (varied), beginning in B major. C.		89. Coda. F.

SECOND MOVEMENT.—"Prestissimo," key of E minor. Sonata Form.

Enunciation.	Development.	Recapitulation.
1 — 24. 1st subject in E minor (tonic). A.		105 — 119[1]. 1st subject in original key. E.
25 — 42[1]. Connecting episode. B.		119[1]—143. Connecting episode. F.
42[1]—66[1]. 2nd subject in B minor. C.	66—104. D.	143[1]—167. 2nd subject in E minor (tonic). G.
		168. Coda. H.

THIRD MOVEMENT.—"Andante Molto Cantabile ed Espressivo," key of E major.

Air with Variations.

Air.	1st Variation.	2nd Variation.	3rd Variation.	4th Variation.	5th Variation.	6th Variation.
	"Molto Espressivo."	"Leggieramente."	"Allegro Vivace."	"Un Poco Meno Andante."	"Allegro ma non Troppo."	"Tempo Primo del Tema."
1— 16. A.	1—19. B.	1—32. C.	1—32. D.	1—2. E.	1—40. F.	1—36[1]. G.
						36. Original Air. H.

In numbering the bars, each portion of a bar, either at the commencement or in the course of a movement, has been reckoned as one bar; the small figures in brackets denote the beat of the bar to which reference is made.

FIRST MOVEMENT.

A. The 1st subject begins with a 4-bar phrase ending in tonic key, bars 1-5[1], followed by another phrase of the same length, ending in the key of B major, bars 5[1]-9[1]. After this it appears as if another phrase were about to commence, but it gets no further than half a bar's length, bar 9[1], before it is interrupted by an episode.

B. This episode, which begins with a discord (inversion of dominant minor 9th), is, after the first 2 bars, in the form of a cadenza; it commences in the key of C♯ minor and ends in B major.

C. The 1st subject is only represented rhythmically and by development (the treble, bars 1-2[1], is in the bass in a different key (B major), bars 17-18[1]). At bar 23[1] a new melody is introduced upon the 1st subject-figure, commencing in G♯ minor. An inverted dominant pedal point, bar 44-50[1], leads to a repetition of the 1st subject in a modified form upon a scale passage in the bass, altered so as to end in tonic key. The perfect cadence, however, is interrupted (as at bar 9-10) by an episode (bar 60).

D. This episode, although it resembles that at letter B, inasmuch as it is formed upon the same figure, is considerably varied both harmonically and melodically.

E. The 1st subject re-appears in the tonic key, varied. At bars 81$^{(5)}$-84 the melody, which appeared at bar 23$^{(6)}$, is referred to.

F. The Coda is constructed upon tonic pedal point and is suggestive of the 1st subject.

SECOND MOVEMENT.

A. The 1st subject may be divided into two parts, both beginning and ending in tonic key. First part, bars 1-8; second part, bars 9-16. The second part, which is constructed upon a dominant pedal point, is repeated with slight additions, bars 17-24.

B. The connecting episode leads off with a 4-bar phrase (in octaves) in tonic key, bars 25-28, imitated and harmonised, bars 29-32, leading to pedal point on dominant of B minor, which is suggestive of the second part of the 1st subject, preparatory to the entry of the 2nd subject, bar 42$^{(6)}$.

C. The 2nd subject for 6 bars is sequential in character, bars 42$^{(6)}$-48. At bar 49 it modulates to C major, and continues in that key until bar 55, where by means of the chord of the diminished 7th on E$\sharp$ (F$\natural$) it proceeds back to B minor, which key is well established by the 4 bars which follow, 57-60, treated in double counterpoint, 61-64. The 2nd subject ends in B minor, bar 66.

D. The development commences with a reference to the 1st subject, the bass of the first 4 bars being adapted from that at bars 59-60 forming a subject which is repeated at various intervals upon pedal point, bars 70-78, resolving itself at bar 79 into C major, in which key, at bar 83, an episode is introduced, which modulates to E minor. The development ends with the dominant chord of B minor.

E. The first part of the 1st subject re-appears in double counterpoint, bars 112-118, the former bass slightly altered, appearing in the treble. The second part of the 1st subject is omitted.

F. The connecting episode is constructed of the same material as before, the beginning being transposed into C major (preceded by a modulation into that key, bars 119$^{(4)}$-120$^{(1)}$). It ends in tonic key.

G. The 2nd subject re-appears with the necessary transpositions, so as to end in the tonic key, instead of in the dominant minor; otherwise it is only slightly altered.

H. The Coda mainly consists of a perfect cadence followed by a passage in contrary motion, the bass of which, beginning at bar 170, is taken from that at bars 158-161.

THIRD MOVEMENT.

A. The "Air" is divided into 2 parts, both repeated; the first part ending on dominant, bar 8, the second part with full close on tonic, bar 16.

B. The interest of the first variation is principally confined to the melody.

C. The second variation is constructed upon a fanciful figure. At bars 9-12 an episode is introduced which appears again at bars 25-28.

D. The time is changed in the third variation from $\frac{3}{4}$ to $\frac{2}{4}$. This variation contains a great deal of double counterpoint. Bars 1-4 are inverted with slight alterations at bars 5-8, and in the same way bars 9-12 at 13-16, and bars 17-24 at bars 25-32.

E. The fourth variation (the time of which changes to $\frac{6}{8}$) is in striking contrast to the preceding variation. It is constructed upon the figure in bar 1, excepting at bars 12-14, which are of a different character.

F. The fifth variation (in common time) is in the fugal style. A subject based upon the original air is answered at the second above for 2 bars in canon with an independent bass. This subject is treated in various ways, the fugal character being maintained throughout.

G. The sixth variation beginning in the original $\frac{3}{4}$ time is a most elaborate one. The beginning of it is like a series of variations upon the first two bars of the air, which are given in almost their former simplicity, bars 1-2. At bars 2-3 the variation is just manifest; two parts in crotchets being changed to quavers. At bar 5 the time is changed to $\frac{6}{8}$ and the accompaniment to triplets of quavers, which alter to semiquavers, bar 6, and to demisemiquavers in $\frac{3}{4}$ time, bar 8$^{(5)}$. At bar 12$^{(3)}$ quite a new form of variation is introduced, which continues for 4 bars, followed by a brilliant episode formed upon dominant pedal point, which is inverted at bar 25, where the second part of the air appears (varied) in the treble.

H. At bar 36 the "Air" is given in its original form, without repeats.

SONATA No. 31.

Op. 110.

FIRST MOVEMENT.—"Moderato Cantabile Molto Espressivo," key of A♭ major. Sonata Form

ENUNCIATION.	DEVELOPMENT.	RECAPITULATION.
1—12[1]. 1st subject in A♭ major (tonic). A.		56—70[1]. 1st subject in original key. F.
		70—87[1]. Connecting episode. G.
12—28[1]. Connecting episode. B.	38—56[1]. E.	87—93[1]. 2nd subject in A♭ major (tonic). H.
28—34[1]. 2nd subject in E♭ major. C.		
34—38[1]. Coda. D.		93. Coda. J.

SECOND MOVEMENT.—"Allegro Molto," key of F minor. A. Ternary Form.

1st Part, key of F minor. 1—42[1]. B.	2nd Part, key of D♭ major. 42[1]—97. C.	3rd Part. 98—147. Repetition of 1st Part. 148. Coda. D.

THIRD MOVEMENT.—"Adagio ma non Troppo." Simple Binary Form.

1—7[1]. Introduction. A.	7[3]—26. B.

FOURTH MOVEMENT.—"Allegro ma non Troppo," key of A♭ major. Rondo and Fugue Form. A.

1st Part.	2nd Part.	3rd Part.
1 — 89[1]. 1st subject in A♭ major (tonic). B.		149[1]—175[1]. 1st subject in original key. F.
89[1] —111. Episode. C.	127[6]—149[1]. Episode. E.	175[1]. Coda. G.
111[1]—127. 1st subject in G major (inverted). D.		

In numbering the bars, each portion of a bar, either at the commencement or in the course of a movement, has been reckoned as one bar; the small figures in brackets denote the beat of the bar to which reference is made.

FIRST MOVEMENT.

A. The 1st subject may be divided into two parts:—the 1st part, bar 1-4, ending on dominant 7th: the 2nd part, consisting of a distinct melody of 8 bars (5-12[1]), ending with full close in tonic key.

B. The connecting episode begins with a brilliant arpeggio passage in tonic key, modulating to the dominant key, in which, after a passage of different character, commencing bar 20, it closes, bar 28.

C. The second subject consists of a passage of 4 bars, extended to 6 bars. The bass of bar 28 is repeated at 29, and also (with one note altered) at bar 30. It begins and ends in the dominant key.

D. A new figure is found at the commencement of the Coda, bar 34, repeated slightly altered, bar 35.

E. The development, after two bars of introduction, is devoted to the first part of the 1st subject, commencing in the key of F minor (bar 40).

F. The 1st subject re-appears, accompanied by a passage resembling that with which the connecting episode begins. The whole of the subject is considerably varied and elongated. The 2nd part, instead of being in the key of the tonic, is, bars 63-66, in the key of D♭ major. At bars 66-70 there is an enharmonic modulation (A♭G♯ and D♭C♯) to E major.

G. The connecting episode begins in E major with the same passage as before; in fact, the whole of it is constructed from the same material, transposed so as to end in A♭ major (tonic), bar 87[1].

H. The 2nd subject re-appears, scarcely altered except harmonically, the key, of course, being changed to A♭ major.

J. The Coda resembles that in the enunciation at the beginning, after a passage of 4 bars, 100⁽ᵐ⁾-104, of a different character, the connecting episode is again referred to; it closes with tonic pedal point.

SECOND MOVEMENT.

A. This movement may be looked upon as a Scherzo and Trio, though not so designated.

B. The 1st part (Scherzo) contains traces of Sonata form. The 1st subject consists of 2 phrases of 4 bars each, 1-8, both ending in dominant major key. What might be called the development, bars 9-29, begins with a sequential passage of 8 bars (9-16), closing in A♭ (relative major), the rhythm being formed by inverting that of bars 5-6. A new figure appears in the relative major, bars 17-21, evidently taken from bars 3-4. A reference to the 1st phrase, bars 21⁽²⁾-25⁽¹⁾, the accent being altered, is followed by the figure at bar 17-18 in the tonic key, leading to the re-appearance of the 1st subject in tonic key, with different accent, as in the development, bar 21⁽ᵐ⁾. It is altered so as to end in tonic key.

C. The 2nd part (Trio) is constructed upon a phrase of eight bars, 42⁽ᵐ⁾-50⁽¹⁾, ending in tonic key (D♭ major). It is repeated with slight alterations, bars 50⁽ᵐ⁾-58⁽¹⁾, ending in G♭ major, in which key it appears, bars 58⁽ᵐ⁾-66⁽¹⁾, repeated, bar 66⁽ᵐ⁾-74⁽¹⁾, slightly altered, ending in E♭ minor. Three bars, 74⁽ᵐ⁾-77⁽¹⁾, lead back to the tonic key (D♭ major), followed immediately by the initial phrase, bars 77⁽ᵐ⁾-85⁽¹⁾, repeated an octave lower, bars 85⁽ᵐ⁾93. Bars 94-97 lead to the repetition of part 1.

D. The Coda simply consists of a few chords in the tonic key (F minor), ending on major tonic chord.

THIRD MOVEMENT.

A. The introduction commences in B♭ minor with a passage of 3 bars, modulating to a cadenza in A♭ minor, and soon afterwards by enharmonic change to another cadenza in E major, which is followed by a modulation to A♭ minor, bar 6, the key of the succeeding movement.

B. Although this movement (which commences at bar 7⁽ᵐ⁾) is in A♭ minor (7 flats), the signature bears only 6 flats. This movement, preceded by the reiteration of the tonic chord, bars 7⁽ᵐ⁾-8, consists of a continuous melody, composed of 4 phrases of 4 bars each. The first phrase, bars 9-12, commences in tonic key, and ends with half-close on the dominant, bar 12⁽ᵐ⁾. The 2nd phrase, bars 13-16⁽ᵐ⁾, commences in tonic key and ends in the relative major (C♭ major). The 3rd phrase, bars 16⁽¹⁾-20⁽ᵐ⁾, begins in C♭ major, and ends with half-close on the dominant of A♭ minor. The 4th phrase, bars 20⁽¹⁾-24⁽ᵐ⁾, begins and ends in A♭ minor, it is followed by a Coda of 2 bars.

FOURTH MOVEMENT.

A. See also Finale, Sonata No. 29.

B. The portion of this movement, which takes the place of the 1st subject, consists of a fugue in 3 parts, the subject of which is announced in the bass; it begins and ends in the tonic key, bars 1⁽¹⁾-5⁽¹⁾. It is regularly answered in the 5th above, bars 5⁽¹⁾-9⁽¹⁾ (counter-subject in quavers). After a short codetta the subject enters in the treble, bars 11⁽¹⁾-15⁽¹⁾, followed by a short sequential episode formed upon the last 4 notes of the subject, ending in the dominant key, bar 20⁽⁵⁾. The answer appears again, bars 20⁽¹⁾-24⁽¹⁾, the subject, bars 28⁽¹⁾-32⁽¹⁾. An episode formed upon the counter-subject leads to the entry of the answer, bars 37⁽¹⁾-41⁽¹⁾, followed by an episode, resembling that beginning bar 15⁽¹⁾, modulating to C minor, in which key a reference to the subject appears in the bass, commencing at bar 48. An episode upon a new subject begins at bar 56⁽¹⁾. The subject enters in D♭ major, bars 62⁽¹⁾-66⁽¹⁾, answered, bars 66⁽¹⁾-70⁽¹⁾. The subject next appears, bar 76⁽¹⁾-80⁽¹⁾, partly answered (in stretto), bar 78⁽¹⁾, and at bar 80⁽¹⁾. The fugue ends upon dominant 7th, bar 89.

C. This episode, with its short introduction (bars 89⁽ᵐ⁾-90), resembles the 3rd movement, transposed a semitone lower into G minor. It is considerably altered, however, and shortened. It ends in G minor, bar 106. The Coda in G major resembles that at the end of 3rd movement (extended).

D. The fugue subject re-appears here, in G major (inverted), bars 111⁽¹⁾-115⁽¹⁾, answered bars 115⁽¹⁾-119⁽¹⁾. Development of it in this form continues till bar 127⁽¹⁾.

E. There is nothing in this movement which takes the place of the 2nd part usually found in Rondo form, unless the episode which begins bar 127 can be looked upon as such. It is formed upon a new subject, bars 127-128⁽ᵐ⁾, in the bass, which is none other than the original subject in diminution. It is treated almost canonically, and with it is combined the subject (augmented), bars 127⁽ᵐ⁾-135, also at bars 135⁽¹⁾-143⁽¹⁾, ending in dominant key. The figure of the foregoing episode gives place to another variation of the original subject, bar 143, which is developed till bar 149. The inverted form of the subject appears at bars 145⁽¹⁾-149⁽¹⁾.

F. The subject re-appears, bars 149⁽¹⁾-153⁽¹⁾, in its original form and key, in octaves, with a new accompaniment, answered, bars 153⁽¹⁾-157. A final entry of the subject, bars 159⁽¹⁾-163⁽¹⁾, followed by a development of the last 4 notes, brings this part of the movement to a close in tonic key, bar 175⁽¹⁾.

G. The Coda principally refers to the 1st subject upon tonic pedal point.

SONATA No. 32.

Op. 111.

FIRST MOVEMENT.—A. Introduction, "Maestoso," 1--17, and Bars 1--3 of "Allegro con Brio." "Allegro con Brio," key of C minor. Sonata Form.

Enunciation.	Development.	Recapitulation.
$4^{(4)}$--$19^{(3)}$. 1st subject in C minor (tonic). B.		$77 - 85^{(1)}$. 1st subject in original key. H.
$19^{(3)}$—34 . Connecting episode. C.	57—$77^{(1)}$. G.	$85 - 101^{(1)}$. Connecting episode. J.
$34^{(3)}$—$39^{(7)}$. 2nd subject in A♭ major. D.		$101^{(2)}$—106. 2nd subject in C major. K.
$39^{(7)}$—$53^{(3)}$. Coda. E.		$107 - 116$. K.
$55 - 56$. F. Double bar and repeat.		117. Coda. L.

SECOND MOVEMENT.—"Arietta," "Adagio Molto Simplice e Cantabile," key of C major. Air with Variations.

Air in C major.	1st Variation.	2nd Variation.	3rd Variation.	4th Variation.	5th Variation.	6th Variation.
1—18. A.	$19^{(3)}$—$37^{(2)}$. B.	40—$57^{(2)}$. C.	59—77. D.	78—110. E. 111—143. Coda.	145—$161^{(3)}$. F. 161--176. Coda.	176—$185^{(1)}$. G. $185^{(2)}$. Coda.

In numbering the bars, each portion of a bar, either at the commencement or in the course of a movement, has been reckoned as one bar; the small figures in brackets denote the beat of the bar to which reference is made.

FIRST MOVEMENT.

A. The introduction commences with a phrase in C minor, ending upon the dominant, bars 1-$3^{(3)}$, which is repeated in F minor, bars $3^{(3)}$-$5^{(3)}$, followed by a passage founded upon the same phrase, which is peculiar on account of the bass forming the complete chromatic scale from G♭ to A♭ in contrary motion with the treble; it comes to a close upon the dominant, bar 12, at which bar a dominant pedal point appears which is continued to the end of the introduction, bar $3^{(1)}$, of "Allegro con brio."

B. The 1st subject begins on the 2nd half of 4th beat of bar 4, preceded by an anticipatory passage, bars 3-4. It is of 2 bars' length, bars 5-6; the last bar is repeated, bar 7; bars 8-9 are a development of the third beat of the 6th bar. Two bars of brilliant passages based upon the chord of the minor 9th lead to a resumption of the 1st subject, harmonised, which, after a passage in contrary motion, ends with full close in tonic key.

C. The connecting episode consists of a fugal development of a varied version of the 1st subject, closing at bar 34 in E♭.

D. The 2nd subject, instead of being in E♭ major, is in A♭ major, bars $34^{(1)}$-$36^{(7)}$; it is repeated (varied), bars $36^{(8)}$-$38^{(7)}$; it ends upon the first inversion of the chord of A♭ major, bar $39^{(5)}$.

E. The Coda, after 2 introductory bars, $39^{(6)}$-41, begins with a 4-bar phrase in A♭ major, bars 42-45, the bass of which is derived from the 1st subject, and is repeated in the treble with slight alterations, bars $45^{(6)}$-$49^{(5)}$. A chromatic passage brings the enunciation to an end in A♭ major, bar 53.

F. Bars 55-56 lead to the development.

G. The development refers principally to the 1st subject. Bars 61-67 consist of a fugal treatment of the 1st subject, which is augmented in one part and in the original time in another. A dominant pedal point (bars 71-75) prepares the ear for the entry of the 1st subject (bar 77).

H. The 1st subject re-appears in double octaves, the second bar (78) is repeated twice (instead of once as before) (bar 79-80), and forms the basis of the next few bars, which resemble bars 16-17, but the full close in the tonic is interrupted, and the passage ends in F minor, bar $85^{(1)}$.

J. The connecting episode is slightly altered and transposed so as to begin in F minor and end on G.

K. The 2nd subject re-appears in the tonic major key, and at bar 107 a prolongation of it begins. The principal phrase occurs in F minor in the bass, bars 109-110 (it is strikingly similar to the beginning of the 2nd subject in the last movement of the so-called " Moonlight " Sonata). A development of the 2nd subject continues till bar 117.

L. The Coda, after 3 introductory bars, 117-119, begins with the same material as in the enunciation, transposed into C minor (tonic key) ; after bar 131, however, it is extended by 4 bars referring to the 1st subject, 131-134, and by a phrase occurring (varied) three times, ending in the tonic major key.

SECOND MOVEMENT.

A. The " Air " is divided into two sections, both repeated. The first section, bars 1-9, commences with a 4-bar phrase, and ends with half-close on dominant, followed by another 4-bar phrase ending in tonic key. The second section, bars 11-18, is also composed of two 4-bar phrases ; the first, bars 11-$14^{(1)}$, in A minor, ending with half-close on the dominant of that key ; the second phrase, bars $14^{(1)}$-18, being in the tonic key. There is no break of any kind between the air and the first variation, or between the variations themselves.

B. The first variation is characterised by a triplet figure in the bass, the melody being written in the same rhythm as the first two notes of the air.

C. In the second variation the time is changed to $\frac{6}{16}$.

D. The third variation is in $\frac{12}{32}$ time, sweeping arpeggios against syncopated chords form the principal feature of this variation.

E. The fourth variation is in $\frac{9}{16}$ time. A great deal of it is constructed upon a pedal point in the bass, see bars 78-85, 95-98, and 99-102. The repetitions of both sections, written out in full, bars 86-94 and bars 103-110, are characterised by the very florid part for the right hand. This variation is followed by a Coda commencing, bar 111, upon tonic pedal point. At bar 120 the perfect cadence is interrupted by the supertonic D being prolonged by a shake, together with references to the "Air." This note (D) at bar 124 is made the leading note to E♭ major, the chord of the 6th on B♮ being followed by the dominant 7th on B♭. This chord continues till bar 128, where the 7th, A♭, begins to rise chromatically to D, the leading note, bar 130, and resolves into E♭ major, bar 132, introducing a phrase of the "Air" (varied) from bars 6, 7, 8, at bars 132, 133, 134. The latter bar is then treated in sequence, bars 134-139, followed by another sequence closing in A♭ major, bars 139-143, succeeded at bar 144 by a diminished seventh on F♯, resolving on the dominant of C major preparatory to the entry of variation 5 in that key.

F. In variation 5 the melody of the air is very prominently given in the treble part against a florid bass. The two sections are not repeated in this variation. At bar $161^{(6)}$ there begins a Coda formed upon the last 3 notes of the air, the final cadence of which resolves into variation 6, bar 176.

G. Variation 6 is constructed entirely upon an inverted dominant pedal point. The air is easily distinguishable ; the first phrase in the inner part, bars 176-$180^{(1)}$; the second phrase in the upper part, bars $180^{(5)}$-184, accompanied by a tremolo bass. At bar 185 a prolongation of the variation commences upon tonic pedal point, which gives place to a passage in imitation, bar 187. Three bars suggestive of the beginning of the "Air" bring this Sonata to a close.

(67)

www.ingramcontent.com/pod-product-compliance
Lightning Source LLC
Chambersburg PA
CBHW021532270326
41930CB00008B/1208